Congress on Trial

Congress on Trial

ꚜꚜꚜꚜꚜꚜꚜꚜꚜꚜꚜꚜꚜꚜꚜꚜꚜꚜ

THE LEGISLATIVE PROCESS

AND THE

ADMINISTRATIVE STATE

By James MacGregor Burns

GORDIAN PRESS, INC.
NEW YORK
1966

For Jan

Contents

Contents

Preface

POKING fun at Congress has become a national pastime. More than any other public institution it is the target of the nation's lampoonery. We find Senator Phogbound in the comic strips and Senator Claghorn on the radio; and the quavering and doltish figure of the confused congressman is part of the cartoonists' stock in trade. Despite their many differences, liberals, conservatives, and radicals agree that the Senate and House often give way to ignoble motives and lose sight of the general welfare. Congress has been called—as Gambetta once branded the French Chamber of Deputies—a "broken mirror in which the nation cannot recognize its own image."

As this is written Congress once again is bringing on itself a storm of abuse and ridicule. The Senate has just passed a new rule that makes the filibuster a more potent weapon for minorities than it has been for 30 years. The majority party's program, endorsed in the last election, is stalled somewhere in the meandering legislative channels, or is being torn to pieces. Once again Congress seems to be parading an insensitivity to public opinion, a tenderness for minority groups, a reluctance to act for the majority of the people. And once again the chasm between President and Congress yawns painfully wide.

Like many Americans I have long been disturbed by the low estate into which Congress seems to have fallen, and curious as to the cause of the trouble. Is the legislative branch merely the people's whipping boy—an easy target because it quarrels and makes laws under a spotlight? Or is it in fact a major weakness in our democracy—even a threat to it? Is Congress a stout weapon for free men—or a vulnerable point in their armor? Or could it be both?

The assumption of this volume is that survival and growth under the harsh conditions of the mid-Twentieth Century require a long, hard look at our governmental as well as our human and natural resources. We seem to live in a time of almost continuous crisis. Yet the real nature of that crisis often eludes us. We know its grim contours—poverty, inflation, unemployment, civil strife, war. We must also understand its causes. These are many; but surely one is the failure of governments to meet and master new problems.

In the United States a government set up in the Eighteenth Century must cope with the trying conditions of the Atomic Age. A government saddled with an artful scheme of checks and balances must try to translate the people's urges into public policies, even when those policies mirror radical shifts in economic and political power. A government long submissive to a dynamic system of private enterprise must itself plan and operate and coordinate vast projects at home and abroad. On the capacity of that government to meet these challenges tellingly and democratically rests the fate of our nation and of large sections of the world.

Our national legislature has carried over into a new era almost unchanged from its character of a century and a half ago. It confronts a powerful President and a huge bureaucracy that shoulders the thousands of tasks of modern government. It confronts a system that may be called the Welfare State, or the Social Service State, or simply Big Government. I use the more neutral term Administrative State—a cluster of controls and services that span the nation and invade almost every area of economic life.

I began to study Congress ten years ago, when I served as legislative assistant to a member of Congress. In following the legislative process since that time I have made use of valuable material in the National Archives, the Library of Congress, and the Franklin D. Roosevelt Library. I am indebted to the following (with their former titles), among others, for firsthand information on legislation that they helped frame: Hugo L. Black, Senator from Alabama; Morris L. Cooke, Administrator of the Rural Electrification Administration; Thomas Corcoran, presidential assistant; John Dickinson, Assistant Secretary of Commerce; Thomas H. Eliot, Representative from Massachusetts; David Ginsburg, general counsel of OPACS and OPA; Albert Gore, Representative from Tennessee; the late Arthur D. Healey, Representative from Massachusetts; Leon Henderson, Administrator of OPA; Meyer Jacobstein, Brookings Institution; Robert M. La Follette, Jr., Senator from Wisconsin; W. Jett Lauck, United Mine Workers; Mike Monroney, Representative from Oklahoma; Randolph Paul, general counsel, Treasury Department; Frances Perkins, Secretary of Labor; Rufus G. Poole, associate solicitor, Department of Labor; Gerard D. Reilly, solicitor, Department of Labor; Donald R. Richberg, Administrator of NRA; Boris Shiskin, American Federation of Labor; Howard W. Smith, Representative from Virginia.

My main debt is to my wife, who has helped me at every stage of writing this book. Max Lerner, my former teacher at Williams College, aided me in trying to put the problem of Congress in broad perspective through his writings and friendly counsel. Pendleton Herring advised and encouraged me in the use of the interview and case study as research techniques. Professors Arthur N. Holcombe and Merle Fainsod of Harvard University advised me in the preparation of studies of the legislative process. David B. Truman, my colleague at Williams, made many valuable suggestions out of his study of group politics in America, as did Stephen K. Bailey of Wesleyan University out of his field work in the effects of local power relationships on national policy-making. I am also indebted to Samuel E. Allen, formerly Professor of English at Williams, for reading the manuscript critically and going over the proofs. I am grateful to all those scholars whose names appear in footnotes and bibliography, and to many whose names do not.

For financial assistance I wish to thank Harvard University, the Social Science Research Council, and (via the GI Bill of Rights) the American people.

J. M. B.

Williamstown, Massachusetts
March, 1949

Congress on Trial

I

The Congressman and His World

O N ENTERING the House of Representatives at Washington, Alexis de Tocqueville wrote over a century ago, "one is struck by the vulgar demeanor of that great assembly. Often there is not a distinguished man in the whole number. Its members are almost all obscure individuals . . . village lawyers, men in trade, or even persons belonging to the lower classes of society."[1]

The young Frenchman sensed that the character of the Representatives told something of the nature of our representative system. His approach is still fruitful today. There is no "average" Congressman. Men and women of many types, reflecting the diversity of American life, make up the mid-Twentieth Century Congress. But what the biologist would call a *type genus*—the member of Congress who best typifies his family—can be singled out for study. He is a composite of those Senators and Representatives who year after year and despite changes in party control determine the make-up of Congress and the main direction it takes.

What is his background? How did he win office? In what does

1. *Democracy in America,* Phillips Bradley *ed.* (New York: A. A. Knopf, 1945), I, p. 204.

he believe? Why will he have national—even international—
significance? For whom does he act?

TALE OF A LOCAL BOY

THE Congressman was born 56 years ago in Boone Center, in
the family dwelling a block off Main Street. His father, who was
raised on a farm east of Boone Center and who as a young man
had moved to town for a business career, owned and operated a
hardware store. Once just a county seat and market center for
the surrounding farms, Boone Center had grown rapidly during
the last part of the century with the establishment of several factories on the east side. The Congressman grew up in a thriving
business community. Although it became increasingly integrated
with the national economy, Boone Center always kept something
of the flavor of a country town grown big.[2]

As a youth the Congressman went to grammar school and high
school in Boone Center. He was president of his class and served
on the debating team that won the state high school tournament
(on the subject: "Resolved: That the farmer, rather than the
businessman, is the main source of American progress"). He
worked one summer in a brickyard—an experience he later made
much of in campaign talks—although he undertook this stint at
manual labor mainly as part of training for the school football
team. Other summers he clerked in his father's store.

At the age of eighteen he left for the law school of the state
university, 65 miles away. This was the farthest he had been from
home, but he was not homesick because the university town was
much like Boone Center, and he associated mainly with his old

2. This chapter is largely based on biographical data; on two studies of the
"country town" by Thorstein Veblen, in *Imperial Germany and the Industrial
Revolution* (New York: B. W. Huebsch, 1915); pp. 315-322, and in *Absen-
tee Ownership* (New York: B. W. Huebsch, 1923); pp. 142-165; and on
studies of communities, including R. S. and H. M. Lynd, *Middletown* (New
York: Harcourt, Brace and Co., 1930) and *Middletown in Transition* (New
York: Harcourt, Brace and Co., 1937); P. F. Lazarsfeld and others, *The People's Choice* (New York: Duell, Sloan and Pearce, 1944); and James West,
Plainville, U.S.A. (New York: Columbia University Press, 1945).

high school friends. Aside from the classics, his studies were almost exclusively in the field of "applied law," and were carefully adapted to the demands of the state bar examination. This examination he duly passed after his fourth year at the university. Boone Center, already an up-and-coming city of 35,000, seemed the most promising place to make a good living; actually, he had never thought seriously of settling elsewhere. For two years he worked in the office of a small law firm before he went into practice on his own. His first client was a realtor who had done business with his father. The young lawyer became a Mason, like his father, and developed a modest but successful practice, with emphasis on trial work.

In 1917 he enlisted in the Army, arriving in France during the late summer of 1918 as an infantry officer. He stayed overseas about a year. Shortly after resuming practice in Boone Center he became active in politics. He was one of the founders of the Bob Davis Post No. 11 of the American Legion. He joined the Elks and Kiwanians and became active in his church (Methodist). He married a Boone Center girl who had been in the class behind him in high school.

After serving as town committeeman of his party for a year, in 1924 he won nomination for assistant prosecuting attorney of the county. Nomination for this office by his party was tantamount to election. He cultivated the party leaders, and his rise in the political hierarchy was steady: county prosecuting attorey; member of the lower house of the state legislature; and, by 1934, member of the state senate. He rose in American Legion circles too, becoming chairman of the legislative committee of the state department and later state commander, taking a year out from his public career to serve in the latter capacity. He won something of a reputation as a liberal in Boone Center when he defended two local AFL building trades officials against charges of extortion.

He moved with his wife and three children in 1935 to a farm on the outskirts of Boone Center. An expert cultivator of good will, he joined the Grange and extended his contacts among the farmers in the region. His new home was, of course, still in his state senatorial district, and it was also in the same Congressional district as before. This Congressional district—the 9th—extended from the retail busines section of his town east through part of the factory and working class region, and after making an unnatural hook north to include the Negro population of a Boone Center suburb, it marched east for thirty miles over broad rich farmland and small townships. The shape of the district resulted from the redistricting of the state by the legislature following the 1930 census; the 9th was gerrymandered so that the party in power, which happened to be the Congressman's, could be expected to prevail by a safe but not excessive margin. In 1938, with the death of the incumbent Representative he was well enough established throughout the district to be the logical successor to the position. Being acceptable to the local party leaders, he was unopposed in the primary, and he won the election without great difficulty.

Today, in his sixth term in the House, the Congressman is in the business of politics, and he is an expert at the trade. He is honest, shrewd, friendly, unassuming, hard-working. He is exceedingly articulate. He knows how to be prudent and conciliatory when the situation so demands, and how to be stubborn. He has a thorough knowledge of the politics and of the business of his district, and of the ties between politics and business. He has an acquaintanceship numbered in the thousands. Although he is not well known outside of his state, the Congressman has been in the House long enough to become one of the more influential members. Because he has an increasingly important role in the formation of national policies, the ideas that move him are of concern to all America.

A CREDO FOR BOONE CENTER

THE Congressman believes firmly that he is a moderate and a middle-of-the-roader. Although he lays no claim to being even a "little left of center," he has abandoned certain ideas that once dominated his thinking. Fifteen or twenty years ago, for example, he believed that the open shop was the American way—certainly the Boone Center way. Today he champions the labor unions in the city, especially if they are not overly influenced by "outsiders."

He accepts governmental activity in fields today that he would have denounced before the Great Depression: price support for farm products; minimum wage standards for workers; old age pensions. On the other hand, planning, governmental paternalism, and centralized power are repugnant to him. America, he feels, is still the land of opportunity for those with initiative and industry, as Boone Center and the 9th District have been for him.

A section of the preamble to the American Legion constitution sums up his political credo, and he likes to quote it at the climax of his speeches: "To combat the autocracy of both the classes and the masses . . ."

Above all else the Congressman believes in Boone Center and the rest of the 9th District. An unashamed booster of the district, he is an expert on its products, its history, and its importance to the nation. He easily becomes sentimental about the "folks back home," and it is honest sentiment. The ancient question as to whether a member of Congress should act for the nation or for his district bothers him not at all. He simply equates Boone Center's well-being with the national welfare. "The people of the 9th District sent me here to represent their interests first," he often proclaims on the floor of the House, but he sees no real issue on that score.

Next to his district, the Congressman believes in his state and in his country. Disdaining the tactics of those he calls "flag-wavers," he nonetheless feels that more Americanism would help solve the problems facing America. He considers himself a "moderate internationalist," having voted for United States membership in the United Nations. He supports American participation in all international organizations, at the same time demanding that this nation retain her full sovereignty. He opposed the loan to Britain on the grounds that America should not bail out socialist governments, and he believes that loans should be made only to nations maintaining free enterprise systems. He is in favor of lower tariffs, but not for foreign goods competing with products of the 9th District.

Part of his Americanism is a latent hostility toward outsiders. Catholics, Jews, and Negroes form small minorities in his constituency, and the Congressman prides himself on his racial tolerance. Indeed, one of his best friends is a Jew. But there is a decided difference in his mind between racial minorities as individuals and as groups. He conceives of minority peoples, especially those in the great urban areas, as tending to harbor alien and un-American ideas. He feels that the amount of racial and religious discrimination in this country is exaggerated, and that the best way to handle the slight intolerance that exists is to ignore it. Making an issue of discrimination simply aggravates it. Incitement to racial and class feeling he vigorously opposes.

Considering that vote-getting is his trade, the Congressman has a curiously ambivalent attitude toward politics and parties. As a practical politician he knows that the daily negotiations and give-and-take are central to the democratic process. Yet he feels that some of the great issues of the day, such as foreign policy, should be kept out of the arena of political conflict. "Politics stops at the water's edge," is a favorite slogan of his.

He is especially critical of party politics in this respect. His own partisanship is a matter of form and little content. Boone Center people are Republican or Democratic nationally, but party ties bind them loosely in local affairs, and the congressional election is considered a matter of local concern. Sane and stable government is possible only if both parties follow a middle-of-the-road course, he believes, and nothing would be worse than a labor party arrayed against a party of business. Although Boone Center has an elaborate class system, he would hate to see politics conducted along class lines.

The Congressman is flatly against "big government." The huge bureaucracy he often pictures as an octopus seated in Washington with its tentacles reaching into every corner of the land. Knowing the many services rendered his constituents, he defends the work of a number of the bureaus, but he looks forward to the day when the trend toward more central government can be reversed. Just how the reversal is to be accomplished he is not sure.

The Congressman distrusts the bureaucrats as a group. They are experts in their fields, while he must be a political jack-of-all-trades. They are theorists and technicians, while he would like to see more "practical" people in government, like himself. Worst of all, they exercise power without having earned the right to do so, he feels. He complains that none of them "could get elected dog catcher" in his home town.

"I am fearful of these experts," he once said on the floor of the House. "The brain trust has cost us money every time it went into action. In my opinion, it will take some farmers from county seats to do the job."

The Congressman is not a man of political principle. He spurns the national platform of his party because it contains provisions designed to appease or attract groups throughout the country in whom he has no interest. But he has no real substitute of his own for such a platform. He has only a bundle of symbols and a sheaf of special claims for Boone Center's organized interests. He believes in Americanism, Democracy, Justice, Freedom, and Patriotism, and he knows why Boone Center needs a new postoffice and why its industries should have more tariff protection and why World War II veterans should have a bonus.

But between the misty symbol and the special plea he takes no stand on the vital national issues on which the presidential elections are at least in part fought out—on taxes and spending, on housing and river development, on full employment and fair employment, on relief and reconstruction abroad, on health and social security. He is no broker of ideas. Indeed, one of his most

effective vote-winning techniques is to evade taking positions on
thorny problems in order not to alienate voters.

How the Congressman steers clear of matters of policy and
principle and sails calm political waters as diplomatic agent of
the 9th District in Washington offers at once a clue to the Congressman's tenacity in office and a lesson in American political
mechanics.

DIPLOMATIC AGENT

THOUGH he may not admit it even to himself, the Congressman's
chief aim is re-election. To stay in office means to gain added
power and prerogatives in Congress on the basis of seniority, and
to become eligible ultimately for higher office—senator, governor, judge, cabinet member. If his re-election depended on successful exploitation of key national issues, the Congressman
would be compelled to run on the record of his votes on those
issues. But his success at the polls hinges largely on how effectively the Congressman has served as the 9th District's representative in Washington. Here his record is almost flawless. He
has rarely faltered in his protection of the sovereign interests of
his locality. Against the encroachments of Big Business, Big
Labor, and Big Government he has defended the rights of small
business, local unions, and the average man in his district. By
seeming to protect the totality of the 9th District's interests
against the outside world, the Congressman contrives to avoid
the basic but perilous issues of national and world policy.

But if the Congressman has little responsibility to his constituents on matters of broad public policy, he has a very definite
responsibility to two groups in the 9th District. One of these consists of the local party leaders—called "bosses" by their opponents—and the other of the organized special interest groups.

The party bosses in the 9th District are concerned almost
wholly with patronage and favors. They are not evil or venal
men; they know that without patronage their political dominion,

centered in city, courthouse, and county machines, would soon crumble. Operating at all levels of American government, they extract from Washington jobs for their followers as postmasters, federal marshals, collectors of internal revenue, judges, and the like. In state and local governments an army of petty officials makes obeisance to the machine for its jobs.

The Congressman advanced smoothly up the ladder from assistant county attorney to his present position only because he never failed to cooperate with his party leaders on matters of patronage. He is fully aware that he needs their support more than they need his supply of federal patronage. For in the case of a falling-out and a showdown—an unthinkable occurrence for the Congressman—he could cut off only one source of their patronage; the bosses would survive to put an end to his political career in the next party primary, over which they exercise a tight grip.

The local party leaders, for the most part, have little interest in the Congressman's votes on national issues. Even when he deserts the national party platform on important legislation, it never occurs to the party leaders that they have any responsibility for that platform. Indeed, the party machine itself often has a bi-partisan slant because of unwritten covenants with the other major party over matters of patronage.

In several cases, however, the local leaders are concerned as individuals, rather than as party officials, with the Congressman's position on certain national policies. A leader of one of Boone Center's wards, for example, is a large lumber dealer, and naturally he is interested in the Congressman's votes on such matters as price control, housing, and subsidies. Two of the county leaders operate large farms and have considerable influence in the Grange; they follow the Congressman's votes on farm bills with care.

The other dominant element in the 9th District—the cluster of organized interest groups—has no concern with patronage but a deep concern with national legislation. The most important pressure groups in the district are those of business, farmers, veterans, and labor, in that order. These groups in turn are made up of individual organizations. The farmers, for example, are divided into the National Grange, the American Farm Bureau Federation, the National Cooperative Milk Producers' Federation, and the Farmers' Union. The veterans divide into the American Legion, the Veterans of Foreign Wars, and World War II organizations. Special issue groups, such as Townsendites and Prohibitionists, take an active part in politics. And there are scores of fraternal, religious, national-origin, and occupational associations.

How many votes do these groups control? The Congressman wishes he knew the answer to this question. With a sharp eye for political margins, he perceives that some organizations lay claim to large memberships, like-minded on all issues, where actually the rank-and-file is small in number, divided, and irresolute. But he cannot be sure. He must feel his way cautiously. Whether or not the pressure groups deliver the votes, they are important media of communication with thousands of voters. The political apathy in his district is often so great that he is unable to "get to" the electorate. The various associations, with their meetings, newspapers, and radio programs, can help him make connections with many voters who might never attend a party rally or read ordinary campaign literature.

Naturally the Congressman tries to gauge the reality of vote-power behind the facade of propaganda. But his responsiveness to the pressure groups is not a matter of votes alone. Often the Congressman makes political decisions without any evaluation of the exact line-up of the various groups back home. He truly "votes his own conscience." If his position happens to coincide with that of the organized groups in his district, it is not simply because he is controlled by them. It is because he is one of them. He is a Legionnaire; he is close to the farmers and their interests; his roots are in the business class. He knows the leaders of the various organizations, and by and large he considers them "sound."

Even the Congressman, with all his political dexterity, cannot act for every one of the groups. To some extent he must choose sides. In practice he speaks for a coalition of groups representing small business, the owners of large farms, veterans of three wars, and skilled labor. He speaks for these groups partly because they are politically effective, partly because he lives in their political world. Thus the business organizations, the Grange, the Farm Bureau, the Legion, the VFW, and the American Federation of Labor carry weight in the congressional representation of the 9th District.

Since even these interests may come into conflict, the Congressman must be able to act for one of them without seeming to flout the claims of the others. Consequently, he moves quickly to confer legislative favors on one pressure group where he can do so without injuring another. He selects his ground carefully. A bonus for veterans, subsidies and price support for farmers, high tariffs for business, the prevailing wage for AFL crafts— such measures are well adapted to the Congressman's use, for not one of them is likely to antagonize the other groups. Tariff protection for the small industries of the 9th District is an especially effective campaign argument because it appeals to both business and labor. Higher farm prices are justified as leading to more spending by farmers in Boone Center's shops. Such measures may mean a higher cost of living for the consumers of the 9th District, but consumers do not make up one of the pressure groups that the Congressman must reckon with on election day.

The Congressman reflects a sense of solidarity in the 9th District that is not wholly artificial. Not only Boone Center but the whole district is essentially a trading and producing community. The operators of big farms, employing machinery and hired hands, must be businessmen as well as farmers. On the local scale there is little disharmony between them and the businessmen of the city. The traders in Boone Center, who were originally independent and self-contained, during the past half-century have increasingly become instruments of a nation-wide commercial system. At one time free agents, Boone Center factories are now

units of a national industrial order. But the myth of the autono-
mous and footloose community still persists, and the Congressman loses few votes in the 9th District when he attacks Wall
Street and Big Business. For the dominant forces in both city
and country have been steeped in the ideas of a local pecuniary
society operating on its own. Militantly conservative, the substantial citizens of the district produce on the local level a gloss
which partially conceals latent conflicts between large and small
business, between business and industry, between workers and
employer, between farm owner and hired hand, between city and
country, between producer and consumer.

The most serious threat to the Congressman's strategy lies in
the dramatization of epochal national questions such as often
dominate the political scene during presidential campaigns. The
exploitation of key issues by a Roosevelt or a Willkie, by a Wallace or a Stassen, draws unorganized voters to the polls and disrupts the united fronts assumed by pressure groups around their
narrow designs. Such issues induce members of even the most
tightly organized groups to forsake their petty interests and to
think and vote in terms of broad national policy.

In such a juncture the Congressman assumes the politician's
protective coloration—he straddles. Refusing to accept the gauge
of battle on the open ground of national policy, he retires into a
defensive zone of evasion, subterfuge, and recourse to "red her-
rings." At all costs he shifts the debate away from his position on
controversial public policy and focusses attention on his fight
for the 9th District and its interests. Here he is on safe ground.

Against the injection of national issues into the local campaign
the Congressman's best defense is the absence of a clear-cut record on those issues. On some important votes in the House there
was no record as to how the members lined up. The Congressman
was not obliged to take a position on some matters because the
bills died in the Senate or in committee. When other bills came
before the House he may have been unavoidably detained on
business in his office or district, and thus unable to vote.

The most effective way to straddle an issue, he has discovered, is to vote on both sides of the question. On one occasion the Congressman voted to kill a bill by recommitting it; half an hour after the recommittal move, he cast his ballot for the legislation. In the case of the price control act of 1942 he advocated a series of crippling amendments, some of which favored manufacturers and farmers in the 9th District, but in the end he voted for the Act. On several occasions he supported measures in Congress only to take part later in "economy drives" that would have starved the agency enforcing the laws. These subterfuges have obvious advantages. In case he is questioned back home as to his stand on these policies, the Congressman can tailor his answer to fit the views of his inquirers and he can point to the record to back up his claims.

If the Congressman were a modern Machiavelli, his advice to freshmen in Congress on "How to Stay in Office" would be: (1) vote for the home folks first, especially for those who are well organized; (2) keep on good terms with the local party bosses; (3) stress your protection of your district's interests as a whole against the outside world; (4) as far as possible do not commit yourself on the important national issues that divide your constituents. But the Congressman is not Machiavellian, and if he gave such advice he would speak in terms of the importance of following a safe and sane middle way, of the dangers of extremism and centralization, of the need for protecting local rights and interests.

CONGRESSIONAL REALPOLITIK

THE Congressman is a member of the House Committee on Banking and Currency. His is an excellent assignment, for this committee is one of the most powerful in the House, handling such matters as fiscal policy, housing, price control, and government lending. Of the fifteen members of his party on the committee, he stands eighth in seniority. The chairman of the committee has been in Congress for twenty years, two years more than the next ranking member. If affairs take their normal course, the Congressman can look forward to heading the committee in another ten years, provided he holds his seat continuously and his party controls Congress when the time arrives.

If the Congressman attains the chairmanship, he will be one of a small company of men exercising far-reaching powers over public policy. His understanding of the committee's subject matter, his political outlook, his ideas on national policy would be of vital concern to the nation. What would be the reason for his rise to such an important position? Not because the other committee members were impressed with his grasp of fiscal matters—whether they were or not, the committee as such has no part in the choice of the man who will be its chief. Not because the House wished to assign him responsibility in this field, for neither do the members of the House have a part in the selection of its committee chairmen.

Even if every other Representative opposed his elevation to the chairmanship he would still take his place, provided he had served enough time, under the inevitable and indisputable workings of the seniority rule. The persons who actually make this decision are the voters of the Ninth District in general and the local party leaders and organized interests of the district in particular—in short, those who send him back year after year to his seat in the House. In the last analysis the chairmen of the House and Senate committees are locally chosen.

Because the Congressman is thoroughly aware of this practical political situation, his main concern will be to retain the favor of the 9th District rather than attempt the role of national statesman. Any prestige he may gain throughout the country will be a secondary factor to achieving popularity at home.

In representing the 9th District at Washington the Congressman must deal with two separate power groups in the House—the party leadership and the committee leadership. The former, elected by the party members, stands for a different constellation of forces from the latter, which holds power simply because of longevity in office. On matters of party procedure and organization in the House the Congressman follows the party leadership. But on matters of public policy he must cooperate with the committee chairmen, for they in turn manage the legislation in which the Congressman is interested. Their capacity for expediting bills advantageous to the 9th District is surpassed only by their ability to thwart passage of those bills. The Congressman knows that they are important people to have on his side.

He defers to the party leadership in the House only when by doing so he will not run counter to the interests of his district or to the undertakings of key chairmen. He operates with a full sense of the allocation of power as it affects him and his constituents. The leaders often take a stand representing a middle position of the party membership, in effect assuming something of a national point of view. The Congressman does not take a national point of view unless it happens to coincide with the predilections of his district, because he is not responsible to a national electorate.

Least of all does he feel that he must conform to the national platform as adopted by his party in convention and interpreted by the presidential candidate. This program, he knows, was written to attract voters in the great industrial states, especially in those states holding the electoral balance of power. The Congressman must operate within an entirely different political context—that of locality. He often greets with suspicion the efforts of the presidential candidates to spell out national platforms in their efforts to win over great masses of votes. In 1940, for example, he differed with many of the forthright opinions of both Wendell Willkie and Franklin D. Roosevelt. And when his party's candidate becomes President, the Congressman feels no obligation to support his policies. He must come to terms with the Chief Executive only if the latter is able, through skilful handling of national issues and of his patronage power, to affect public opinion and political forces in the 9th District.

Thus the grand strategy of congressional politics requires that
the Congressman keep in mind the immediate interests of his
own district first, last, and most of the way between. Accordingly,
most of his time is taken up not with matters of national policy
but with doing odd jobs for the politicians, pressure groups, and
average voters of the 9th District. He is part promoter, part er-
rand boy. He spends hours each week acting in effect as counsel
for business firms and other groups before federal administrative
agencies. He must try to find jobs every year for hundreds of the
home folks. He must deal with thousands of requests each month
for aid in getting satisfaction from the agencies.

Letters and telegrams pour into his office with personal problems that take hours of his or his staff's time to solve. Many of
his constituents visit him with requests for favors, many others
telephone him. Most of the time, in short, he is immersed in
trivia. He knows that satisfying these requests is the best insur-
ance for re-election. He believes, moreover, that he must help
humanize the often impersonal relationships between citizen and
bureaucrat.

"There are Congressmen elected year after year," Walter Lippmann has written, "who never think of dissipating their energy
on public affairs. They prefer to do a little service for a lot of
people on a lot of little subjects, rather than try to engage in
trying to do a big service out there in the void."[3] The Congressman ideally fits this picture.

Given the political and human situations involved, it is not
surprising that the Congressman finds little time to be a legislator. He takes his intellectual nourishment in snatches—half an
hour at a committee meeting in the morning, a few minutes lis-
tening to debate in the House following a quorum call in the
afternoon.

His brief case bulges with elaborate reports from the administrative agencies, with briefs from interest groups, with independent studies, all of which he hopes to examine but which he

3. *Public Opinion* (New York: The MacMillan Company, 1922), p. 247.

will have time to skim at most. He is in steady retreat before the constantly rising burden of private business, the never-ending task of satisfying local needs and interests.

At times the Congressman has a sense of his own inadequacy in attempting to tussle with vast and intricate questions of international and domestic policy on the basis of such limited study. But he is reassured by the thought that common sense, of which he has a full store, can solve most of these problems.

The Congressman's world, then, is largely confined within the boundaries of the 9th District and is shaped by the business spirit and way of life of Boone Center. It is a world where old ideas and myths still survive, blurring the alignments that economic and political forces inevitably produce. As the champion of his world, the Congressman defends it against its real and imaginary adversaries outside. As the product of his world, he puts its imprint on congressional action.

II

ЛЛЛЛЛЛЛЛЛЛЛЛЛЛЛЛЛЛЛЛЛ

The Pressure Politicians

WE HEAR much of lobbyists and pressure groups, but a curious myth persists as to their role in American politics. According to this myth, the member of Congress arrives in Washington eager to work for the national welfare, or at least for his constituents. He is ready to stand by the grand political principles that he expounded on the platform and as a result of which he received a majority of the votes. But trials and temptations beset him at the nation's capital. Greedy lobbyists for big business invite him to Bacchanalian feasts, where they seek to influence him with cash and chorus girls. Scores of labor lobbyists swarm through the corridors, buttonholing him and his colleagues and demanding legislative favors. He is mercilessly belabored and bedeviled by other pressure groups. If he is a good Congressman, he will reject all bribes and threats. If he is not, he will soon give in to cupidity and timidity.

This is a picture, in short, of unscrupulous lobbyists and of single-minded legislators. The trouble with the picture is that most lobbyists are discreet and honest men, while many Congressmen themselves are little more than lobbyists in disguise.

PRESSURE POLITICIANS AT WORK

THE Congressman, as we have seen, represents not merely an amorphous collection of persons in a particular area. He is spokesman for the organized interests at home in their economic and political jousts with groups outside the district. Every member of Congress has a keen sense of the dominant economic enterprises in his district, whether he comes from a cotton-growing region in the South or a steel-producing city in the mid-West or a textile-making area of New England or a cattle-raising county of Montana.

The common term for organized special interests that exert influence on government is "pressure groups." Yet it would be to miscalculate the power and methods of organized minorities to say that the major groups in a district need bring "pressure" on a Congressman. Most Congressmen do not wait for pressure from home. They take the initiative, moving to protect the interest group before any pressure is in sight. They are ready with their arguments, their amendments, their parliamentary strategy the moment the interests back home seem to be endangered. As active propagandists, they convert their offices into temporary headquarters for a politically mobilized group. They are in fact lobbyists, but they work at the core of government rather than at the periphery. They are the makers of pressure, not merely the subjects of it. They are pressure politicians.

Some of the pressure politicians in Congress serve interest groups far more effectively than lobbyists could possibly hope to. Consider, for example, Representative Robert L. Doughton of North Carolina, who was for many years chairman of the House Committee on Ways and Means, and one of the chief policymakers in tax matters and other national legislation. During consideration of the revenue bill of 1943—a measure of vital national importance—he made clear more than once[1] that the tobacco grower in his district was "the man in whom I have my

1. *Hearings on Revenue Revision of 1943*, 78th Congress, 1st Session, House of Representatives, pp. 199, 293.

first interest." Doughton was able to scuttle an Administration move to increase taxes on cigarettes, cigars, chewing and smoking tobacco, and snuff. Watching this performance with admiration, a Republican legislator told representatives of tobacco interests: "While the tobacco farmers may not have a representative in this city, they have an excellent friend in the Chairman of this Committee, who is not only familiar with the problems of the farmers, but he watches out for their interests."[1] There was no evidence that tobacco farmers put "pressure" on Doughton. They did not need to.

Some members of Congress are so zealous in protecting special interests that their nicknames carry the mark. Years ago Representative William D. Kelley of Pennsylvania was known as "Pig Iron" Kelley for his unceasing fight to gain tariff protection for a leading enterprise of his district. More recently we have had "Cotton Ed" Smith, who helped organize the Southern Cotton Association in 1905 and who never wavered in his fight for the cotton growers of his home state of South Carolina. The links between other members of Congress and dominant interests at home may be less obvious but they are no less important.

The great task of the pressure politician is to induce his colleagues to see things his way. Some of them, of course, already are won to the cause by virtue of the pressure groups in their own constituencies. Other Congressmen come from areas where those groups may be less powerful. With them the pressure politician may attempt the traditional bartering of legislative favors. This is known as log-rolling, or the process under which, as one Washington lobbyist puts it, "You scratch my back and I'll scratch yours."

The pressure politician also works closely with the lobbyists or "legislative agents" of the group supporting him. The alliance of lobbyist and pressure politician is an effective one. A publicity campaign is launched as the cause, however narrow, is elevated into a great moral or patriotic issue. An association headed by

1. *Ibid.,* p. 1517.

respectable leaders is set up. Citizens with local influence are brought to Washington to appeal personally to their representatives. A vast letter-writing and telegram-sending campaign is organized. The pressure politicians in Congress carry the campaign to the floors of the House and Senate and to the committee sessions with speeches and briefs. All media of publicity are exploited—radio, press, cinema, public forums, even schools and colleges.

Where aid from lobbyists is not available the pressure politician himself may actively recruit organized support. He may stir into action a slumbering interest group with dire warnings as to the effect of proposed laws. He may decide to take certain legislative action and then organize support at home for such action. Such activity is quite the reverse of the usual idea of "pressure politics."

Representatives of organized groups, whether members of Congress or not, follow two basic rules. One rule is to claim boundless support throughout the nation for a given policy, no matter how small a group would benefit from that policy. As Schattschneider says, "Never admit that it is only you who is talking."[3] The other is to equate one's special interest with the national interest or the general welfare.

Spokesmen for sheep raisers argue that artificially supported wool prices will ensure a domestic supply of wool in the event of another war. Industry representatives assert that higher tariffs will benefit labor through increased wages, as well as help business. Organized labor pleads that extended social security programs will stabilize the economy along with safeguarding the less privileged. Whether true or not, such avowals would shift the argument from the area of crass group interest to the level of a higher morality and patriotism.

Witness a small incident taking place on the floor of the Senate on January 15, 1944. An important war-time tax bill is under

3. E. E. Schattschneider, *Party Government* (New York: Farrar and Rinehart, 1942), p. 200.

consideration, and one clause provides for a tax on furs and fur coats. Senator John H. Overton of Louisiana has just introduced an amendment to this clause exempting fur garments costing $150 or less from the new rate. He is doing this, he says again and again, for the sake of "poor struggling girls" who need to "protect themselves against the winter's blasts."

Other Senators object and tempers flare. Senator Champ Clark of Missouri, who has voted for the fur tax in committee, shouts that Overton "walked toward me and shook his fist at me and accused every member of the committee who voted for this provision . . . of being in league with a gang of manufacturers for the purpose of trying to render naked a lot of deserving girls who wanted to wear fur coats. . . . It almost breaks my heart to contemplate the pathetic picture drawn by the Senator from Louisiana of the poor, freezing girls in semi-tropical Louisiana being harassed and bedeviled because they are not able to wear these necessary fur garments for their protection from the cold."[4]

What was behind this performance of Overton's? Perhaps he was genuinely concerned about working girls who lack fur coats. More likely he was thinking of the fact that over 20,000 trappers, fur buyers, and fur dealers in Louisiana specialized in cheap furs retailing for less than $150, and would be affected adversely by the proposed tax. Here was a special interest in camouflage.

Lobbyists always seem to be in public disfavor. Most of the states regulate their activities; the Georgia constitution outlaws lobbying altogether, and Alabama has made lobbying for or against a measure a misdemeanor. In the Legislative Reorganization Act of 1946, Congress provided for the registration of organized groups and their legislative agents, and for the filing of detailed accounts of their receipts and expenditures. This provision was designed to enable Congress and the public to judge the claims of lobbyists in terms of the pressure groups they represent.

Congress has done nothing, however, about those of its members who are in effect lobbyists in disguise, although former Rep-

4. *Congressional Record,* January 15, 1944, pp. 234, 236, 237.

resentative Robert Ramspeck of Georgia took a step in that direction when he proposed a constitutional amendment forbidding Congressmen to deal with the executive branch except on legislative matters. Disguised lobbying is by far the more serious problem.

Few lobbyists try to conceal the fact that they speak for certain organizations. Testifying before a congressional committee a lobbyist will identify himself as national legislative representative of the Brotherhood of Railway Trainmen, or chairman of the Spinach Committee of the Baltimore Canned Foods Exchange, or vice-president of the Westinghouse Electric Corporation, or managing director of the Northeastern Poultry Producers' Council. There can be little doubt as to what and whom these spokesmen represent. Can one say the same of legislators who pretend to speak for the national interest, or at least for their constituents as a whole, and who in fact are acting for a pressure group?

THE PHYSIOLOGY OF PRESSURE

PRESSURE groups are powerful chiefly because they invade and envelop our regular political processes. This is the hard fact that we hate to accept. Any good democrat prefers to think that organized special interests gain their ends through trickery and dishonesty rather than through the democratic process. To be sure, the pressure groups sometimes stoop to questionable methods. But generally they are effective because they play the political game expertly and tirelessly.

Half a century ago the "interests" had a different basis of power. One spoke casually of the "oil" and "silver" and "railroad" senators who were the puppets of the industrial and financial giants of the day. These captive-congressmen owed their jobs to huge corporations that had little "ballot power" but enormous "dollar power." In politics, as in business, money talked. Whole legislatures were corrupted, officials were bought and sold by the job lot, governmental favors were purchased in vast financial transactions. From the Yazoo land frauds through *Crédit Mobilier* and the Harding oil scandals the men with cash to dispense have made their arrangements under cover of the patriotic outcries of the politicos.

Money is still a potent factor in politics, but today it is used mainly to sway elections rather than as a direct means of influencing politicians once the votes are counted. The strengthening of democratic machinery by such devices as the direct primary system of nomination, the direct election of Senators, and curbs on political activities of corporations, has forced the special interests to prove their power at the polls. Many members of Congress are still the creatures of pressure groups, but they owe their positions to the strength at home of an organized group as a whole, rather than to a few manipulators at the top. We still speak, for example, of "silver senators" but they are likely to represent the whole industry and not merely a handful of mine owners.

The Anti-Saloon League gave the classic demonstration a generation ago of how a superbly organized minority group could put over its program by cultivating its strength at the polls. The League carefully observed the three cardinal rules of effective minority politics: (1) Organize voting power in the members' constituencies; (2) maintain a legislative office to keep pressure on Congressmen with tendencies to waver; (3) never let the membership become divided over side issues. The League's great weapon was not bribery or propaganda as such, but its actual or vaunted power at the polls. "The surest way to secure needed temperance legislation," declared a League strategist, "is for the sovereign voters, through well planned organization, to elect men as their representatives ... who will write the laws upon the statute books." This formula worked. It was reported that the average Congressman feared the League more than he feared the President of the United States.[5] Considering how hard it is to amend the American Constitution, the adoption of the 18th

5. For the full story of the Anti-Saloon League, see Peter H. Odegard, *Pressure Politics* (New York: Columbia University Press, 1928).

Amendment was the ultimate tribute to the organized political strength of the Anti-Saloon League.

At the opposite pole from a high-powered group like the old League are the associations that have representatives in Washington but no strength throughout the states and districts. The "People's Lobby" is such a group. Benjamin Marsh, its director, regularly appears before congressional committees to testify in behalf of unorganized Americans. The committee members listen to him politely and duly incorporate his briefs in the committee's record. Some day historians may judge that Ben Marsh had the wisest suggestions of all the persons who appeared; certainly the low-income groups for which he speaks deserve representation before Congress. But it seems unlikely that the "People's Lobby" ever influenced an important decision in House or Senate. It would be hard to find a better example of the powerlessness of ideas in Congressional politics without organized power to back them up.

The strength of pressure groups lies only in part in the conscious mobilization and channeling of votes. Indeed, many organizations refuse to choose openly between candidates in order to protect their "nonpartisanship." Their influence may appear in more subtle ways. In most groups there are leaders and followers. The former are opinion-moulders, and they influence their followers in hundreds of casual face-to-face conversations.

These personal contacts often affect voting behavior to a greater extent than do even the press or radio, for the contacts are frequent, the "opinion leader" in the group is usually trusted, the argument can be tailored to suit the biases of the follower, and the follower is probably less "on his guard" against absorbing opinions than when encountering formal media of communication, such as the press or radio.[6] As Lazarsfeld has pointed out, voting is essentially a group experience, and people vote with—and for—their group.[7]

6. P. F. Lazarsfeld and others, *The People's Choice* (New York: Duell, Sloan and Pearce, 1944), Chpts. 15 and 16.
7. *Op. cit.*, p. 148.

Even so, the voting power of pressure groups is often exaggerated. The rank-and-file of every organized minority is subject to a variety of sectional, occupational, religious, family, and other influences which cause the members to desert the group in the privacy of the ballot booth or to stay home on Election Day.

Unfortunately, the congressman himself is only too prone to do the exaggerating. But can one blame him? He has few ways of testing the group's voting power or the solidarity of its members. For the most part he deals with the group leaders, who naturally picture their followers as broadly and enthusiastically united. Trying to garner votes from an electorate that is erratic and nebulous and apathetic and often adrift, he naturally clutches for the support of groups and group leaders who are approachable and purposeful and who can swing at least a few votes in his direction.

The pressure groups, moreover, can speak with a loud voice. Many congressmen count their mail in an effort to see how the wind is blowing back home. Pressure can be turned on overnight. Price Administrator Chester Bowles once estimated that 5000 telegrams poured in on members of Congress in two days from automobile dealers seeking exemption from an OPA regulation. Many a congressman would like to resist "government by telegram," but he must be careful. Pressure groups have long memories. And they are articulate about legislative detail. The votes on amendments and the parliamentary maneuvers that might escape the attention of the average voter are spotted by the lobbyist sitting in the gallery.

The decisions of the important groups—the Cotton Textile Institute, the Legion, the CIO, the National Association of Home Builders, the NAM, the Grange, and so on—are front-page news, but the smaller, local organizations are important too. It is extraordinary how trifling an organized special interest may seem to be and still enjoy representation in government. The late Charles L. Gifford, who represented the Cape Cod area of Massachusetts in the House of Representatives, commented on this situation during debate over the price control bill in 1941.

"If a legislator is sent here from a 'bean' section," Mr. Gifford said, "he will—and seemingly must—protect beans. His constituents demand it to be his first interest. Difficult it is for most to sacrifice themselves and their 'bean' constituents. If one thinks politics easy, 'try sitting top of a high rail fence and keeping one ear close to the ground.' "

Mr. Gifford himself, however, had striven mightily to protect fish from the rigors of price control, for his 9th Massachusetts district had hundreds of miles of coastline. "I was very much interested in the gentleman's discussion of beans," declared Representative Merlin Hull of Wisconsin. "I wonder if the gentleman would not go a little further and take up the matter of fish."

"Yes, I will," replied Mr. Gifford. "I trust that I may have a little political sense. I asked that fish and fishermen be granted about the same consideration as the farmers. This was most cheerfully granted. However, no fishermen or fishermen's organization appealed to me. . . . But, of course, I should expect to watch over their interests when others are getting theirs."[8]

One cannot blame Mr. Gifford for protecting his fishermen. Watching over their interests was part of his duty. If he had failed in that duty, he would ultimately have been replaced by someone who could defend the interests of the district. Even Abraham Lincoln won his election to the Illinois legislature partly as a result of demanding a canal from the Sangamon River to aid his constituents, according to his law partner.[9] Nor can one pass judgment on the leaders of pressure groups. Inevitably those leaders will seek to bolster the group's economic position with political power, for they know that in a world of hotly contending groups, and in a society coming to be increasingly administered by government, their economic strength may ebb away if they have not the political vigor to back it up.

One can, however, pass judgment on a political system that lets pressure politics get out of hand. In a free society pressure

8. *Congressional Record,* January 26, 1942, p. 671.
9. E. Hertz, *The Hidden Lincoln* (New York: The Viking Press, 1938), p. 64.

groups are inevitable and desirable. But there must be limits. "If we do not eliminate selfish abuse of power by any one group," declared President Dwight D. Eisenhower in his inaugural address at Columbia, "we can be certain that equally selfish retaliation by other groups will ensue."[10]

DEMOCRACY'S EXPOSED FLANK

LIKE an army probing for the enemy's weak point, pressure groups search out the sector of government that is least hostile to the attainment of their ends. In the United States that sector is held by the legislative branch. As between the chief authors of over-all national policy—Congress and President—it is the former that shows itself far more responsive to the drives of organized minorities. In times of sharp political conflict the Senate and the House, dominated by pressure politicians and their allies, over and again become deploying areas for mobilized pressure groups.

This is not to say that these groups operate only through Congress. Some administrative agencies have long been known for their close kinship with organized interests, which influence appointments, policy-making, policy execution. Nor is it to say that the President himself is oblivious to pressure groups. No political leader can be. But while the Chief Executive, dependent for support on a majority of the whole nation, can gauge the voting power behind the groups with a certain perspective, Congress tends to dissolve into a congeries of blocs and individual legislators who are unwilling and unable to withstand the organized minorities. Indeed, the responsiveness of many administrative agencies to minority pressures is partly a result of control by Congress over agency personnel and funds.

Striking evidence of congressional weakness in the face of organized minorities, and of presidential firmness, can be found in the story of veterans' bonus legislation. Presidents Warren G.

10. *New York Herald Tribune*, October 13, 1948, p. 15.

Harding, Calvin Coolidge, Herbert Hoover, and Franklin D. Roosevelt each had the experience of vetoing bonus bills, only to have the House pass them over those vetoes. In none of the four cases did more than 90 Representatives out of 435 vote against the veterans' groups. The American Legion and the other veterans' organizations scored these signal successes because they were organized locally in states and districts. Although a minority, they made up for lack of numbers by working energetically for these special ends. They showed how to play the minority game.

Who represented the American people as a whole in these cases, President or Congress? There is no evidence that the pro-bonus Representatives suffered at the polls. But neither did the anti-bonus Presidents. The veterans' groups were never able to make the bonus an issue in the presidential campaign, but they succeeded in making it a factor in many congressional campaigns. This experience with bonus bills tells us little about the respective personal virtues of the Chief Executives and the Congressmen: the four Presidents felt that they would gain more by vetoing the bills than they would lose, and the Representatives believed that the safer course was to vote for them. This experience does illuminate our strange representative system, under which Congress responds to an entirely different set of forces than does the President.[11]

How explain this contrast between President and Congress in their response to pressure groups? The key to it lies largely in the manner in which they are elected—that is, in the underpinnings of their political power. As suggested in the previous chapter, organized minorities have a more significant role in congressional elections than in presidential. In the former contests the public issues are usually less well defined, national problems receive less emphasis, protection of local interests becomes a central question, and the organized voters exercise relatively greater

11. For further discussion of the bonus bill cases see E. E. Schattschneider, *Party Government* (New York: Farrar and Rinehart, 1942), pp. 194-196; and V. O. Key, Jr., "The Veterans and the House of Representatives," *Journal of Politics,* Vol. V, No. 1, pp. 27-40.

weight. All these conditions strengthen the position of the pressure groups.

The presidential candidates, on the other hand, argue issues that often transcend the petty claims of the special interests. To be sure, they must handle with care the appeals of organized minorities, but at the same time they need not fear that any pressure group could make its demands a prime issue in the national campaign. For if any such attempt were made, the group would be swamped under by the far larger number of voters, organized or not, who would resent wholesale capitulation to special interests. In the case of the veterans' bonus bills, for example, not one of the subsequent rivals of the anti-bonus presidents made the veto an issue in the presidential campaign. To have done so would have won the support of some veterans only to have jeopardized the support of millions of non-veterans.

Viewing the situation from the Congressman's vantage point, one sees why it is not so easy for him to withstand the pressure groups. In the first place, his state or district may be so dominated by one or two interests—such as tobacco-growing, mining, or automobile-manufacturing—that he can aspire to no greater standing than that of the out-and-out pressure politician. But often he must submit even to the smaller pressure groups. For the disciplined rank and file of the organized special interest knows how to influence local sentiment and deliver the votes, while usually the mass of the voters can be counted on only for indifference or irresolution.

"The apathy of the many, in the face of the enormous complexity of our economic and political structure, is the common premise of all pressure groups," Max Lerner has said. "With it as a given, they are able through their condensed urgencies to translate their minority interest into a psychic majority."[12]

But the translation is a false one, as Lerner points out. The minority wields power only because the majority has abdicated. Indeed, it is astonishing how much representation in Congress

12. *It Is Later Than You Think* (New York: Viking Press, 1943), p. 113.

can be gained by a small but well distributed pressure group. John Gunther, noting this phenomenon while traveling through the states that maintain the sugar bloc in Congress, wrote: "Only 3 per cent of American farmers grow sugar beet and cane; the entire processing industry employs no more than twenty-five thousand people. But sugar is spread through many states—beets grow in seventeen, cane in two—which gives it thirty-eight senators out of ninety-six, and they can certainly make a noise."[13] The President, elected by millions upon millions of voters, can assign the proper weight to the sugar growers and processors, and similar pressure groups.

Thus Congress occupies our government's exposed flank, against which the small but disciplined forces of the special interests take the offensive in order to invade the citadel of political power at the expense of the majority of the people. It is no accident that representatives of organized groups are called the "third house of Congress." Nor is it surprising that such measures as price control—the bulwark of consumers and other unorganized people—were continually under attack in Congress and finally dismantled there; that passage of the Taft-Hartley Act was the signal for labor to renew its efforts in congressional elections; that sectional minorities like the South, and occupational minorities like the farmers, receive their greatest political representation nationally in House and Senate. The pressure politicians and their allies hamstring action by the majority, and to the extent that popular government rests on majority rule, they are a threat to democracy.

13. *Inside U.S.A.* (New York: Harper & Brothers, 1947), p. 221.

III

ЛЛЛЛЛЛЛЛЛЛЛЛЛЛЛЛЛЛЛЛ

The Impotence of Party

IN THE United States, as in any political democracy, an immense medley of interests competes for power and for the rewards that go with power. These interests are of many types, ranging from a large but ill organized group like the Protestants to a small but locally influential association like the Rotary Club; from great power groups like the CIO to more specialized outfits such as the Non-Smokers Protective League of America. The power they seek takes many forms—influence over the administration of a city ordinance, or the monopoly of a commodity, or the staving off of governmental intervention in some field, or the setting of a tariff rate, or control of a county relief program, or even mastery of the whole machinery of government.

The interests may be economic, ideological, racial, religious, fraternal, occupational, or some other; but in most cases they have, consciously or not, a political role as well.

The struggle for power among the more formidable of these groups is sometimes waged far below the surface of national affairs. Sometimes it is front-page news. That struggle may take place in lawyers' chambers, in an editorial office, in a courtroom, in a politician's or administrator's office, at a meeting of a board of directors, in the convention of a political party, in a "smoke-filled room." Or it may erupt in picket lines, strikes, race riots, pogroms, civil war. The struggle may be at least temporarily resolved at the polls or in pitched battle; or it may not be resolved at all.

The conflict among such groups would lead to anarchy were it not for powerful forces for harmony and cooperation. These forces stem from the awareness of most groups and persons that only by working together can men achieve their goals. It is this awareness that separates civilization from chaos. Men join in groups to pursue their mutual ends, and groups work together to achieve their broader purposes. Thus workers form unions; unions join forces in state and national associations; and associations of unions consolidate in an AFL or CIO. Similarly with business, agricultural, occupational, veterans, and many other types of groups. Lesser differences are submerged for the sake of a broader agreement.

There is, at least in the political world, a limit to this process of combination. At some point the compromises and concessions implicit in joint operations seem too costly to the group, or at least to the dominant elements within it. Thus businessmen are divided among the Chamber of Commerce, NAM, and many independent groups; farmers among the National Grange, Farmers' Union, American Farm Bureau Federation, and the like; union men and women among the AFL, CIO, railway brotherhoods, and other combines; veterans among the Legion, VFW, and World War II outfits—to name only a few of the divided interest groups in the nation. Religious and fraternal associations are also fragmentized.

To give a show of unity the group leaders may arrange for tentative alliances, marriages of convenience, liaison committees, clearing houses, and the like, especially when they are on the defensive. Yet there is no real unity. Like dancers in a vast Virginia reel, groups merge, break off, meet again, veer away to new combinations. But social harmony cannot long continue amid the dizzy fluctuations of minority groups. At long last it requires the affirmation of a basic concurrence on the part of a majority of the people, and machinery to express that concurrence.

OUR MULTI-PARTY SYSTEM

IF THE thousands of organized interests in a democracy reflect these group antagonisms, it is the two-party system which, under ideal conditions, exploits the underlying solidarity among people. It is that system which, functioning properly, manages to express the concurrence of a majority.

How does the two-party system accomplish this vital task? The answer is not hard to find. In any democracy a major party seeks control of the government. To achieve that goal it bids for support throughout the community. To gain that support the party must broaden its platform through a series of compromises with organized groups and with unorganized voters. No narrow program will do the job. Constantly searching for the beliefs that bind diverse groups, the party's policy-makers define the issues that transcend the claims of special interests and find response among great masses of the people. Since the politicians attempt to attract as many "customers" as possible, the party system becomes, in the words of Lord Bryce, "the best instrument for the suppression of dissident minorities democracy has yet devised."[1] For in a democracy the parties can hold a minority in check without stifling its creative function in the polity.

In the United States especially, a major party must find the common denominator among a large and varied group of voters, for it hopes to pluck the biggest plum of all at the next election— the Presidency. To elect a Chief Executive it must produce an electoral majority, and in doing so it forces adjustments among minority groups. As Carl Becker has said, "the fundamental compromises are, in the first instance, made not between the major parties but within them." Once having gone through this process of compromise in each of their camps, the two parties can offer the voters a relatively simple "either-or" choice rather than a confused array of alternatives. The two parties take up new ideas and attract new voters in order to survive in rigorous competition,

1. *Modern Democracies* (New York: MacMillan, 1921), Vol. II, p. 44.

and in doing so they display the inclusiveness that is central to democracy.

Such, ideally, are the benefits of a two-party system. But in the United States we do not enjoy these benefits because our two-party system breaks down in the legislative branch. What we have in Congress might better be called a multi-party system. Instead of a grand encounter between the rallied forces of the two great parties in House and Senate, the legislative battle often degenerates into scuffles and skirmishes among minority groups. On matters of vital public policy the major parties fail to hold their lines. They leave the field in possession of the pressure politicians and other members of Congress who are faithful to a locality or to a special interest but not to the national platform of their party.

A glance at virtually any House or Senate roll call will demonstrate the inability of the party to enforce discipline even if it should try. In recent years the Democratic party has been especially vulnerable to the disruptive effects of bloc voting, but the Republicans too are rarely able to prevent at least a few of their adherents from crossing party lines. Party irresponsibility also affects the shaping of bills in committee and on the floor before the final roll call is reached. Indeed, it is hardly proper even to use the term "party responsibility" in discussing Congress, for the most rudimentary underpinnings of such responsibility do not exist. The party members in Congress have no common political program; as Pendleton Herring has said, "On the majority of issues the party takes no stand."[2] And if there were such a program, little machinery exists in House or Senate to enforce it.

As a result of this situation we have in Congress, as far as public policy is concerned, a group of splinter parties. They are the Southern Democratic party, the Farmers' party, the Labor party, the New Deal party, the Liberal Republican party, the

2. *Presidential Government* (New York: Farrar and Rinehart, 1940), p. 29.

Veterans' party, the Silver party, and many others, along with the faithful adherents of the Republican and Democratic parties. A President of the United States is a Democrat or Republican, but key Senators and Representatives are more than likely to vote as members of a multi-party system.

This congressional patchwork is neither new nor accidental. It is rooted in American political organization. As national institutions, our parties are decrepit. They are coalitions of state and local party organizations, pulling together in awkward harmony every four years in an attempt to elect a President, going their own way the rest of the time.

The bosses who run the party machines are concerned more with private spoils than with public policy. The pressure groups that work through and around the parties are interested in their own designs, which may or may not coincide with the general welfare.[3]

Lacking central control and discipline, the major party cannot hold its congressmen responsible to the broad majority of the voters in the nation who put the party into power. The national committee and chairman of the party have little control over national policy. They can do nothing for the congressman—he feels no responsibility to them.

Senators and Representatives can blithely disregard the national political platform; if they bother to pay it lip service, they usually do so because the program is so broad as to permit the widest leeway. In their states and districts the congressmen are responsible to fragments of the party—fragments that assume a variety of shapes under the impact of economic, sectional, ideological, and other forces.

BRITAIN: PARTY GOVERNMENT IN ACTION

WE HAVE much to learn from the English on this matter of political organization in a democracy. For over the course of many years they have forged a system of party government in the full

3. See Schattschneider, *op. cit.,* esp. chpts. IV-VII.

sense of the term. That system serves three cardinal purposes. It unites the various branches of the government in order to carry out the will of a popular majority. It staves off the thrusts for power of minority groups. And as recent events have made clear, it offers the voters a genuine choice between two fairly distinct programs, rather than the Tweedledum-Tweedledee alternatives that often characterize political encounters in the United States.

The British party system leaves the member of Parliament with what seems to some Americans a shocking lack of independence. While in this country the congressman blandly wanders back and forth across party lines, in England cross-voting on the part of major party representatives is unusual. While here the Senator or Representative as policy-maker juggles party principles with alacrity, or often ignores them entirely, the M.P. faithfully votes the party program as interpreted by the Cabinet. While the member of Congress often wins votes as a result of his independence, the member of Parliament deserts his party at grave peril to his chances of re-election.

The difference between the British system and ours is not, of course, one of personality, but one of basic political organization. There the party is supreme. Its role in national life is so meaningful and decisive that most Englishmen vote in terms of the party program and record, rather than on the basis of the personality, salesmanship, and promises of the individual candidate. They judge the office-seeker by his party label. They do not elect Tom Brown or Sir Wyatt Smith, but the Labour or Conservative candidate.

And the victor at the polls discovers that the party ties are even firmer once he has taken his place in the House of Commons. Often, in the words of Winston Churchill, he "becomes a silent drudge, tramping at intervals through lobbies to record his vote, and wondering why he comes to Westminster at all."[4] Ordinarily the most that the private member will do—in the rare case when he is so inclined—is merely to abstain from voting

4. *Life of Lord Randolph Churchill,* Vol. I, pp. 69-70, quoted by Ivor Jennings, *Parliament* (New York: The MacMillan Company, 1940), p. 342.

on an issue. He may have fought hard for his point of view within the party councils, but once the party has made up its mind on an important matter, he is expected to go along.

On first look such a scheme might seem to bear an authoritarian stamp. But in fact the British party system is an almost ideal form of representative government. By forcing candidates for Parliament to run on the national platforms, it gives the voter a real choice between two opposing programs. And the voter expects the successful candidate to support that program once he takes his seat in the Commons, for faithfulness to that cause is part of the bargain between voter, candidate, and party. The parties make no pretense of responding to every ripple of public opinion, or to every pressure of some organized minority. They have the more vital function of expressing the broad political aspirations of a majority of the people. While in this country Congress often seems to represent every group except the majority, in Britain the major parties, operating at the highest level of political organization, give the national welfare right of way over minority interests.

Despite the omnipotence of party in Britain, the legislature is not a dead letter. On the contrary, Parliament enjoys enormous prestige in that country and throughout much of the world. "It has occupied the centre of the political stage for centuries," Jennings has written. "So much of the history of freedom is part of the history of Parliament that freedom and parliamentary government are often considered to be the same thing."[5] The situation is not paradoxical. The prestige of Parliament rests squarely on the robustness of the bi-party system. With that foundation Parliament enables the Cabinet to provide the leadership that is essential at a time when democracy is under pressure from inside and from without, and it equips the Opposition with the means to attack the government in open forum. Without that foundation Parliament would be as impotent and as suspect as the assemblies in multi-party states.

5. *Op. cit.*, p. 502.

How to explain the contrast between party domination of the legislative in Britain and the constant disruption of party lines in Congress? The answer, in part, lies in the greater homogeneity of the British people that permits a more cohesive political structure. But that is not the whole answer, for Britain too has her sectional rivalries that cut across parties, her special interests that would use either party in their quest for influence. The main reason for that contrast is the organization of political power in Britain as compared with America.

The Conservative Party, and to an even greater extent the Labour party, are centralized agencies. Ample control over funds, program, and the choice of candidates is lodged in the national office of each party. Because each is responsible for judgment and action on a national scale it requires its parliamentary members to vote in national terms. In contrast to the loose decentralized party structure of the United States, continually disintegrating in Congress under the impact of organized minorities, the British parties have the means of holding their M.P.'s in line.

It is not a matter simply of enforcement machinery. Discipline in the British party rests also on the fact that, except perhaps in times of fast-moving political developments, its program is a genuine compromise among the various groups making up the party. That program is carefully devised not only to consolidate the support of the rank and file but to attract independent voters as well. On the theory that an M.P. is more easily led than driven, it may even make concessions to local and sectional interests. But those concessions are never so fundamental as to endanger seriously the party's loyalty to its national program. It is precisely in this respect—at least as far as discipline in the legislative body is concerned—that the American parties differ so drastically from their British counterparts.

MAKE-BELIEVE MAJORITIES

LACKING the party rule that invigorates the British parliamentary system, Congress is often unable to furnish majorities for

even the most urgent measures. While Parliament automatically
musters enough votes to enact the program of the party in power,
or else must face dissolution, the majority party in Congress cannot control its own rank and file. Hence bills in Congress get
stymied in committee; they survive in one chamber only to stall
in the other; a few fail in conference between Senate and House.
When measures become marooned somewhere in the winding
legislative channels, the villain of the piece may well be a minority group holding a strong position in committee or chamber,
and the majority may be powerless to come to the rescue.

How, then, do bills get passed? Partly as a result of the appeals
and threats of a President acting as chief legislator as well as chief
executive. The President's control of patronage, his means of
mobilizing public opinion, the authority of his office often enable
him to drive measures through the legislature. In many cases, too,
legislation is enacted largely as a result of bi-party coalitions responding to group pressures of some sort. Such important measures as the McNary-Haugen proposals for farm surplus control
in the 1920's, the Smoot-Hawley tariff of 1930, the Economy
Act of 1933, the National Industrial Recovery Act of the same
year, the Employment Act of 1946, the Greek-Turkish aid bill
of 1947, to name only a few, were passed by Congress as a result
of bi-party support.

Least significant of all in the enactment of legislation seems to
be the party as such. Half a century ago A. Lawrence Lowell set
out to discover how often more than nine-tenths of the party
members in Congress voted on the same side of a question. He
found such party cohesion in less than eight per cent of the important bills considered by the Thirty-Eighth Congress, elected in
1862; and party influence on legislation was even less in other
samples he studied.[6]

Party cohesion is still slight today. And as for straight party

6. "The Influence of Party Upon Legislation in England and America,"
American Historical Association, Annual Report, 1901, Vol. I, p. 323.

voting—where every Republican lines up on one side of an issue and every Democrat on the opposite side—it would be difficult indeed to find an example of such voting on an important issue (aside from "organizing" the House or Senate) in the last quarter century.

In the absence of party voting Congress at times falls back on curious methods of producing majorities. One of these might be termed the "majority by threat." It is the most primitive of all means of securing a working combination. Rather than agreeing on a common program, blocs threaten to withhold their votes from bills backed by other blocs unless support is forthcoming for their own.

It is a sort of log-rolling in reverse, with the advocates of a measure saying in effect: "If you dare to vote against our bill, we will vote against yours." Thus in 1937 the labor bloc in Congress threatened to oppose agricultural legislation unless farm representatives supported a wages and hours bill. In considering the price control bill of 1942 the majority leader issued a similar warning to the farm group. There is a vast difference between such attempts to win votes through fugitive alliances in reverse, and the effecting of agreement by intra-party action based on awareness of a broad but genuine identity of interest.

Another crude method of achieving joint action on bills is "evasion by delegation"—the consignment of broad powers of decision to the President when congressional blocs cannot agree on a closely defined policy. Not because of the need for administrative discretion but because of its own failure to find a basis for agreement, Congress passes important policy-making powers on to the Chief Executive.

An example of such delegation is found in the consideration of the National Industrial Recovery Act in 1933; protectionist and anti-protectionist Senators were at odds over an embargo provision, and as a "compromise" they left the matter to the discretion of Mr. Roosevelt. This type of delegation is a form of legislative abdication.

Such behavior by congressional majorities should not be confused with genuine majority rule. It is one thing for a party to present its platform and candidates to the voters and, when vested with power, to make specific policies in terms of the approved program. It is quite another matter when bi-party majorities, operating without the endorsement of a majority of the voters, capture the machinery of law-making. Such majorities in Congress raise hob with the representative process. They have little responsibility to the people. They may gain their ends and disappear overnight. Their actions may be good or bad, but in either case the bi-party coalitions can ignore with impunity the national party platforms which, however vague and irresolute, at least must pass some kind of public inspection. Bi-party blocs cannot long provide real majority rule. The fleeting majorities that they muster are often not truly representative of the majority of the voters.

If these coalitions do not provide real majority rule, what does? In a democracy majority rule is assumed to be the best means of discovering and satisfying the "public interest." But what kind of majority? There are many types—the majority required to pass an amendment to the Constitution, that needed to push a bill through Congress, that involved in electing a President, and others.

The most democratic, stable, and effective type of majority, however, is a popular majority—namely, one half of all the pooled votes throughout the nation, plus one (or more). This is a different sort of majority than that represented by a coalition in Congress responding to minorities organized in the various states and districts. "No public policy could ever be the mere sum of the demands of the organized special interests," says Schattschneider; ". . . the sum of the special interests, especially the organized special interests, is not equal to the total of all interests of the community, for there are vital common interests that cannot be organized by pressure groups."[7]

Not only do pressure groups often fail to represent fairly the interests of many of their own members. Also in the interstices of the pressure groups one finds voting fragments that see their main stake in the well-being of the community at large. The marginal members of pressure groups, those who are not members of pressure groups, and the voters who are torn between allegiance to competing pressure groups—all these have significant weight in a nation-wide popular election, but far less weight in the sum total of local elections. In short, they are far more influential in choosing Presidents (even with the electoral college) than in choosing members of Congress.

Consequently, a popular majority tends to be more representative and democratic than a "segmented" majority. It is more stable too, because it cannot be manipulated by a few pressure politicians who are able to mobilize organized interests in various states and districts. A simple, mass, nation-wide, popular majority is often feared as leading to the "tyranny of the majority." Actually it is the safest kind of majority. Building a nation-wide coalition of twenty or more millions of voters is no mean feat. It requires the presidential candidate to find a basis of harmony among diverse groups and to widen his platform to attract those groups and the millions of independent voters. A popular majority, like democratic politics in general,[8] furnishes its own checks and balances.

The nation-wide political party is the natural vehicle for a popular majority. But it is also a rickety one. "Coalition fever" in Congress reflects the weakness of the American parties—their inertia, their slackness, their fear of assuming leadership. Organ-

7. *Op. cit.,* p. 31; see also P. H. Appleby, *Big Democracy* (New York: Alfred A. Knopf, 1945), p. 134, and Adolf Sturmthal, *The Tragedy of European Labor* (New York: Columbia University Press, 1943), pp, ix ff.

8. H. S. Commager, *Majority Rule and Minority Rights* (New York: Oxford University Press, 1943), pp. 57 ff.

ized interest groups display precisely the traits that the parties should display but do not—discipline over their representatives in office, alertness, the capacity to submerge internal differences in a united drive toward the more decisive group objectives. The special interests operate through either or both major parties with a cynical disregard for the party platform. "In a Republican district I was Republican; in a Democratic district I was a Democrat; and in a doubtful district I was doubtful," said Jay Gould, "but I was always Erie."

Similarly with the organized interests of today. It would be inconceivable for a dairy Senator from Wisconsin, a silver Congressman from Colorado, a cotton Senator from Alabama to desert their respective groups to uphold the party platform or the general welfare. In a Congress lacking sturdy party organization, many of the nation's pressure groups seem to enjoy greater representation than the majority of the voters.

THE PERVERSION OF POLITICS

SOME believe that the impotence of party in Congress is altogether desirable. They fear that a disciplined party system would smother the expression of dissenting points of view, would choke off all opinions unacceptable to either of the major parties. In the independence of the Congressman from party control they see a bulwark against party autocracy.

Such fears of party despotism are largely groundless. To win elections—especially to win the Presidency—a party must attract voters of so many diverse political views and allegiances that its program of necessity will be broad and general, except in a case where the people are hopelessly split over some irresolvable issue. In the drawing up of the party program and in the interpretation of it, there is room for the expression of many diverse views. Candidates using the party label to win votes should be expected to operate within the general boundaries of the party program after they are elected. Their failure to do so undermines majority rule, for that failure is often a sign not of independence, but of subservience to organized groups at home—groups that may form a small minority of the whole electorate.

Party irresponsibility in Congress has at least two serious implications for American democracy. The first is linked closely with the nature of our government. That government is still today, as the Founding Fathers in 1787 set it up to be, a system of checks and balances. It is still nicely contrived to maintain that "separate and distinct exercise of the different powers of government, which to a certain extent is admitted on all hands to be essential to the preservation of liberty."[9] The President has a limited veto over congressional action; either house of Congress can thwart a presidential program; and the Supreme Court has at least a suspensive veto over the executive and legislative branches. Minority groups that could not possibly elect a President have found that they could work through the House, Senate, or Supreme Court.

A government divided within itself has been tolerable during most of our history, because it has not been called upon to shoulder major burdens except during war. Of recent years, however, the people have turned to the national government, even in peacetime, for more vigorous and extensive action. Sensing that private enterprise could not alone insure full employment and economic stability, they have turned to the only other agency that had the resources to tackle that job. Doubtless that tendency will continue. But if there is no way to harmonize the separated organs of government, sustained and effective action may be impossible.

It is that vital function of integration that the majority party ideally should fulfill. Operating through both branches of Congress and through the committees as well, having as its chief the occupant of the White House, not without influence even in the judicial branch, the majority party should be the perfect instrument for carrying out a popular mandate. But if the party can-

9. *The Federalist* No. 51 (Hamilton or Madison).

not enforce its will in House and Senate, it fails to meet a vital need of American national government.

A second consequence of their weakness in Congress is to make parties seem meaningless and even dishonest in the mind of the public. When a member of Congress ignores his party's promises the questions arise: Does the party really mean what it says, or is its program simply a means of enlisting popular support without assuming responsibility for action? Are party members holding office servants of the people or political mountebanks? A further misgiving—the most serious of all—arises: If Senators and Representatives of one party vote frequently with their "colleagues across the aisle," is there any real distinction between the two parties? Or are the donkey and elephant twins under the skin?

During a time of tranquillity this question is hardly more than an academic one. Indeed, many voters, instead of decrying the absence of a clear-cut majority party and opposition party, actually like their parties to be similar in both objectives and methods. To them that similarity seems to prove the solidarity of the American people. But in a time of rising social tensions and sharp group conflict the voters may refuse to go along with an arrangement that has the earmarks of a one-party system. They will seek alternatives, and the vital question is whether our party system will have sufficient vigor and flexibility to provide those alternatives, or whether alternative policies will lie outside the compass of the party system.

When the people feel like voting out the "ins" and voting in the "outs" it is essential that a party be ready with a different program from the repudiated one. But if both parties are committed to the existing scheme of things, the electorate will reject both. They may turn to a third party, or they may resort to movements that would provide authoritarian ways of dealing with emergencies that the existing parties were unable to master. In that event, the failure of the party system leads to failure of democracy itself.

For democracy can fail, and largely as a result of its political organization. Léon Blum recognized this fact. In his prison cell in the fortress of Pourtalet the great Frenchman, a veteran of years of parliamentary warfare, assessed the causes of his country's collapse. He recalled the "useless din of oratory, the slowness of procedure, the successive encroachments and mutual usurpations of legislative on executive and executive on legislative; the group rivalries and personal quarrels, the weakness and precariousness of ministries without backing or staying power, imagination or courage. . . ." He concluded that the parliamentary system of government in France needed radical modification in the direction of party government.

"If the parliamentary system has succeeded in England and failed in France, it is essentially because there exists in England a strong and established party system . . .," Blum wrote. "Ministerial instability, the flaccidities and vacillations of governments, the failures and fitfulness of parliamentary debate—in short, the breakdowns and irregularities of the French parliamentary machine—are in the first place the consequence of the absence of disciplined and homogeneous parties."[10]

Ultimately, then, the impotence of parties in a democracy puts a blight on the whole political process. Men come to expect the great decisions to be made outside the government they control. They come to regard all politics—and especially party politics—as at best a farce, and at worst a fraud. They become skeptical of the political method of responsible compromise as the indispensable method of democracy.

How often do we find editors, columnists, radio commentators, even politicians themselves arguing that a controversial issue should be "kept out of politics," that a president or congressman is "playing party politics," that public policies should not be dealt with in a "spirit of partisanship." Early in 1948, for example, the Republicans accused President Truman of "politics" following

10. *For All Mankind,* trans. by W. Pickles (New York: The Viking Press, 1946), pp. 59, 64.

his annual message to Congress, and newspapers solemnly concluded that it was a "political" talk directed toward the 1948
election.

Surely this is a remarkable attitude in a democracy. How else
would we have problems resolved? By officials who were not
"political"? By politicians who were not thinking of the next
election? By leaders who were not trying to please the people?
The people may be wrong, but who is more likely to be right?
In a democracy we must have politics; we must have party politics and party politicians. In no other way can a democracy handle the contentious issues that constantly arise in a free society.
Party politics as such is not at fault, for it permits people to live
together somewhere between anarchy and absolutism.

The trouble lies in the perversion of politics—the use of political methods to deceive the people, to dissipate their energy, to
destroy their will to action. Politics is perverted when politicians
fail to live up to the promises of their party. It is perverted where
the one-party system flourishes, as in the South, or where the
minority party is a captive of the dominant organization, as in
many boss-controlled cities. It is perverted by what Harold J.
Laski has called the "inherent erosion of principle"[11] that attends
the efforts of politicians to represent minorities rather than the
majority. Without a party system that defines and attacks national problems on behalf of a majority of the voters as a
whole, politics and politicians become the corrupters of democracy rather than its custodians.

11. *Parliamentary Government in England* (New York: The Viking
Press, 1938), pp. 57, 59.

IV

Houses of Misrepresentatives

CONGRESS, we are told, is the heart of representative government, the citadel of American democracy. Such a claim is more an expression of faith than a statement of fact; yet it contains an important element of truth. Congress is democratic and representative in the sense that its members reflect the sentiments of numberless minorities throughout the nation. It serves democracy's vital need for a national forum where sectional protest, local aspirations, will-o'-the-wisp ideas, and even the bunkum of everyday politics, can find an outlet.

But Congress should be more than a sounding board for minorities. As the seat of legislative power it has the equally important job of representing a majority of the voters as a whole. To serve as instruments of majority rule the Senate and House must mirror—and act on—the sentiments of a popular majority.

It is precisely here that Congress subverts representative democracy. For various reasons that we will examine, both the House and the Senate are defective as "representative" bodies. And they both are organized and managed so as to yield to organized minorities at the expense of the great majority.

THE ROTTEN BOROUGHS

EVEN before Governor Gerry of Massachusetts in 1812 carved

Essex County into a salamander-shaped district, thereby disconcerting his Federalist opponents and inspiring a new phrase, Americans had come to accept with cynical amusement the manipulation of election districts for unfair party advantage.

Gerrymandering is still part of the "political game." Our states and cities show the cumulative effects of the handicraft of politicians who have known just how to spread the majorities of their own party over as many districts as possible while concentrating their opponents' strength in as few districts as possible. This device often leads to strange deformities in the representative process. In the 1928 Maryland election, for example, more voters chose Republican than Democratic candidates for Congress, but Maryland sent four Democrats to Washington and only two Republicans.

The curlycues that appear on election maps are as bizarre as the election results. In the outlines of a Kentucky district a federal court once found a remarkable resemblance to a "French style telephone." "Shoe-string" and "saddle-bag" districts are common. Occasionally a long thin finger stretches out from an otherwise symmetrical district to include a single ward of a city.

"If you let your imagination go while thumbing through the maps of Congressional districts," Volta Torrey says, "you may readily fancy that you have seen a dumbbell, a tomahawk, a skull, a worm, the M-G-M lion, and characters from the comic strips."[1]

This kind of gerrymandering is only one part of the problem of unfair representation. Even more serious is automatic gerrymandering—the inequalities that result from the failure of districts to be adjusted to shifts in population. Although arithmetical accuracy is out of the question, all congressional districts in a state are supposed to be roughly equal in population. In fact they often vary widely, for some states have not redistricted since the turn of the century, and others are at least a decade or two behind.

1. *You and Your Congress* (New York: William Morrow & Co., 1944), p. 31.

Today, in 14 out of the 44 states that have more than one Representative, the population of the largest district is more than twice that of the smallest. Such "gerrymandering by default" leads to the incongruous situation where one citizen may have a third or even an eighth of the voting power of another citizen living a short distance away. This condition brings to mind the famous "rotten boroughs" of England, where a half-submerged town like Dunwick, with 14 voters, had two members of parliament, while great cities such as Birmingham had none.

Here are some of the consequences of unequal apportionment: In 1932 there were no less than eight states in which a party polling less than half the congressional votes elected a majority of the members. In the 1932 and 1936 Massachusetts elections, Republican candidates for Congress polled hardly ten per cent more votes than Democratic candidates, but the Bay State sent ten Republican Representatives to Washington and only five Democrats.[2] In 1930 more West Virginians voted Democratic than Republican in the congressional elections, but four Republicans were victorious and only two Democrats.

The immediate causes of "rotten boroughs" may vary greatly. Gerrymandering can be used to hold competing groups in check, as in the efforts of Chicago bosses to hold down the voting power of the Poles or Italians, or of prohibitionists to pare that of the "wets." But the long-run effect of unfair districting is more significant than such shenanigans. It is to endow rural minorities with far more political power than their numbers justify and to discriminate against city dwellers by reducing their voting strength.

Over many decades there has been a shift of population in the United States to urban areas, but not a proportionate shift in voting strength. State legislatures control districting, and most legislatures over-represent rural areas. In Connecticut, for example,

2. This result was due also, of course, to the workings of the single-member district system.

70.4 per cent of the people lived in cities, according to the 1930 census, but the cities had less than one-fourth of the representation in the lower house in 1936.

Discrimination against urban areas might not be serious if there were agreement between city and country dwellers over basic issues. Unfortunately there are basic differences. Industrial labor, the main interest group in most urban areas, often clashes with agricultural groups over such matters as price control, wage and hour regulation, the rights and duties of organized labor, governmental subsidies, and the like. Producer interests are stronger in rural areas, consumer interests in urban areas.

Other questions that often divide country and city are liquor control, taxation, relief, and public works.[3] Broadly speaking, discrimination against the city means discrimination against the Democrats, except in the South. Alfred E. Smith complained at New York's constitutional convention in 1938:[4]

... when I campaigned through this State, I campaigned against as good men as the Republican party could put up, and we talked these issues; and each time that I won, I was inaugurated, and the next day the Republican Speaker was elected, and then they came down to talk to me about their platform—a platform that had been thrown out of the window, repudiated, cast aside by the electorate of the State. That is what happens under an unfair apportionment.

Aroused by glaring inequalities in Illinois, where one congressional district had a population of 112,116 and another had over eight times that number, three citizens of the state in 1946 turned to the federal courts in an effort to gain fair districting. They asserted that the existing arrangement abridged their privileges as citizens of the United States, denied them equal protection of the laws in violation of the Fourteenth Amendment, and violated the guaranty of a republican form of government. A district court

3. See V. O. Key, *Politics, Parties, and Pressure Groups* (New York: Thomas Y. Crowell Co., 1942), pp. 552-564.
4. Quoted by Key, *ibid.*, p. 558.

expressed sympathy with their cause but ruled against them because of a previous Supreme Court decision.

The three plaintiffs—a political scientist, a professor of law, and an attorney—thereupon appealed to the Supreme Court. That court, badly divided, also ruled against them. Justice Frankfurter, for the court, declared the question to be a "political" one which the judicial branch had not the authority to settle. Dissenting, Justice Black, joined by Justices Douglas and Murphy, asserted that the court could—and should—intervene when a system of "rotten boroughs," to use Black's words, led to "gross inequality in the voting power of citizens" and to a denial of equal protection of the laws.[5]

Justice Frankfurter held that the remedy for unfair districting lay with the Illinois legislature, with Congress, or ultimately with the people. This advice was scant consolation for the victims of unfair districting. To appeal to state legislatures would be fruitless; present districting arrangements are considered eminently satisfactory to those in power. In some states even the state constitutions fortify the system; thus the lower house in New York has been called "Republican by constitutional law."

Nor does Congress offer much hope. It has power under the Constitution to require fair districting in congressional elections, and its apportionment acts of former days provided that districts be "compact" and "contiguous." But Congress, itself under the bias of mal-apportionment, never enforced these injunctions, and even the formal requirements have been dropped in the last two apportionment acts. Perhaps the remedy lies with the people— but through what agency can they act?

It may seem somewhat academic to worry about over-representation of rural areas in the House when the Senate is the citadel of the "acreage" states. The results of unfair congressional districting do seem trivial indeed when one Nevadan, mathematically at least, has the influence of 100 New Yorkers in the upper

5. Colegrove *et al.* v. Green *et al.*, No. 804, Oct. Term, 1945; decided June 10, 1946, 66 S. Ct. Rpt. 1198.

chamber. That is unfair representation *par excellence*. But the problem cannot be minimized by compounding it.

The Senate was set up to speak for the states equally and today it over-represents the rural population; the House was to speak for people equally (except for slaves) and today it also over-represents rural groups. The net result is a deformity in the representative process that has been troublesome in the past and may be dangerous in the future.

THE COURT-BARONS

"POWER is nowhere concentrated," Woodrow Wilson wrote of Congress. "It is divided up, as it were, into forty-seven seigniories, in each of which a Standing Committee is the court-baron and its chairman lord-proprietor."[6] These words ring as true today as when Wilson wrote them sixty-five years ago.

Deluged each session with thousands of bills, hundreds of which will complete the legislative journey, Congress must delegate most of its policy-making. Committees can speed bills along their way or kill them outright; they can amend them beyond recognition, or pigeonhole them, or quietly bury them. Whatever they do, their decision is usually sustained on the floor. They are, as Speaker Reed once observed, "the eye, the ear, the hand, and very often the brain of the House"—and his remark applies to the Senate as well.

In view of the power of these "little legislatures," one might expect them to be truly representative of the body for which they make policy. But such is not the case. Far from being faithful miniatures, some committees are dominated by spokesmen for particular sectional or economic interests.

Thus in 1946 all the members of the Senate Committee on Mines and Mining, with one exception, had substantial mining interests in their states. Not one member of the Senate Com-

6. *Congressional Government* (15th ed.; Boston: Houghton Mifflin Company, 1900), p. 92.

mittee on Irrigation and Reclamation came from the populous Northeast. Not one member of the Senate Committee on Agriculture and Forestry represented a primarily industrial or urban state, and only four of the twenty members of this committee were from urban-rural states. Fourteen of the eighteen members of the Senate Committee on Naval Affairs spoke for states with salt-water coastlines. In 1937 O. R. Altman found that "a large majority on Finance, the tax and tariff committee, represent industrial states of the North and East."[7] A similar situation existed in House committees; the great bulk of the membership of Agriculture, for example, has represented rural districts.

It is only natural for Congressmen to seek membership on the committees that affect the major interests of their constituents. But the result is that many committees tend to use their power to the advantage of special interests. They come to represent blocs in Congress rather than the Senate or House as a whole. Lobbyists for special interests cluster about them. Wilson spoke scornfully of the "interested persons who walk attendance upon the Committee on Rivers and Harbors."[8] The history of such legislation as the recent Missouri Valley Authority bill (see Chapter Five) shows how that and similar committees could still be made to serve minority ends.

As a result of being reshuffled and "streamlined" in the 1946 reorganization of Congress, some committees became more representative, but others remained out of focus. The Senate Committee on Agriculture and Forestry was made sensitive to farm interests to an even greater degree than before the reorganization. Every member of the Senate's new Public Lands committee spoke for states west of the Mississippi, and most of them for the Rocky Mountain area. The House Agriculture committee was as narrowly composed as before. In 1947 all but one of the members of the Merchant Marine and Fisheries committee in the

7. "First Session of the Seventy-Fifth Congress," *American Political Science Review*, Vol. XXXI, No. 6, Dec. 1937, p. 1076.
8. *Op. cit.*, p. 190.

lower chamber represented districts on the coasts of the Atlantic, Pacific, Gulf of Mexico, or Great Lakes.

Nor did the reorganizers dare to meddle in the seigniory of the Rules committee, which still stood as the most powerful and the most irresponsible organ of the House of Representatives. Any large assembly needs a traffic officer to direct the stream of bills and resolutions and to see that the most important measures receive right of way. The members of the Rules committee had this function—and much more. They could veto a bill by refusing to report it. They could amend measures as the price of permitting them on the floor. They could substitute a wholly new measure for the one framed by another legislative committee. By providing legislation with a "wide-open" or with a "gag" rule they could gravely affect its chances of surviving intact on the House floor.

George B. Galloway described Rules as a "governing committee ... able to advance directly, or to retard indirectly, any measure which it selects for passage or slaughter."[9] Its members may even alter the powers and privileges of other committees.

Yet the Rules committee has little responsibility to the House or to the majority party. Until 1910 the Speaker was its chairman and helmsman, and he was able to use it as an instrument of the party controlling the House. With his dethronement the committee lost its only formal link with the majority, and Rules was left adrift on the seas of sectionalism and localism. Under the present system the members stay on the committee as long as they remain in Congress; they need answer only to the voters back home. They can defy the President, the House leadership, and public opinion with impunity, and they have often done so.

In January, 1949, the Democratic leaders in the House won support for a new rule designed to clip the wings of the Rules committee. The House voted that after Rules had sat on a bill for 21 days, the chairman of the committee reporting the bill might call it up before the whole House. The change was a step forward, for the Rules committee could no longer bottle up a

9. *Op. cit.,* p. 112.

bill indefinitely. But its other powers remained, such as the control of the handling of a bill on the floor. And most of the power lost by Rules seemed to have been shifted to committee chairmen rather than to the House leadership.

The Rules committee is dominated by veteran congressmen who have been reelected time and again regardless of the ebb and flow of national politics. Consequently, it is often out of touch with popular sentiment.

After the 1936 election, for example, five anti-New Deal Democrats held the balance of power on the committee, and the most influential of these—Cox of Georgia, Smith of Virginia, and Dies of Texas—loathed the progressive program of an Administration that had just won a sweeping endorsement throughout the nation. The committee proceeded to raise hob with the President's measures. The chairman, John O'Connor of New York City, was so hostile to the New Deal that President Roosevelt intervened personally in O'Connor's next primary fight in a successful effort to defeat him. In 1948, seven of the eight Republicans on Rules were from rural constituencies, and three of the four Democrats; thus this "governing committee" afforded little representation to the millions of urban voters in the nation. Originally designed as a tool of the majority, the Rules committee has become the instrument of minorities.

THE LORD-PROPRIETORS

AMONG the most influential members of Congress are the chairmen of the important Senate and House committees. As in Wilson's time, these "lord-proprietors" are masters within their bailiwicks. "They arrange the schedules of work and the agenda of committee meetings," a group of political scientists reported in 1945. "They parcel out the personnel of subcommittees and determine the scope of their work. They or their subordinate chairmen of the subcommittees report to Congress on decisions for legislation and manage the floor debates in defense of such decisions. In these debates the committee chairman's word carries great weight because the subject is his peculiar province. In effect, the committee chairmen are able in large measure to dictate what proposals for legislation may be considered by Congress. The ordinary member proposes, but the chairman disposes."[10] These are not extravagant words.

The chairmen have a decisive voice in determining how policies shall be considered; inevitably they have great influence on the policies adopted. Who are these key policy-makers? They are of many different types, but they are alike in one respect. They are all products of the seniority system in Congress. They have come to power solely because both House and Senate award chairmanships to committee members with the longest uninterrupted tenure on the committees. They are the "old-timers" of Capitol Hill.

It is more instructive to see what the chairmen are not. They are not necessarily the choice of the committee they head, for the committee has no power to choose its own chairman. They are not the choice of the House or Senate as a whole, nor of the members of the majority party in either house, nor of a committee or presiding officer elected by Congress. None of these agencies has any influence over the appointment of chairmen; thus the chairmen have no responsibility to any of these agencies. In the last analysis, these pivotal makers of national policy are responsible only to those states and districts that return them to Congress. They are "locally chosen and locally responsible."[11] No matter what else they do—or fail to do—they will rise to power if they cultivate the home folks.

The effect of the seniority system is to vest disproportionate power in those states and districts that tend to reelect their Congressmen. Although there are many individual variations, a recurring pattern is discernible. When Democrats control Congress

10. *The Reorganization of Congress,* A Report of the Committee on Congress of the American Political Science Association (Washington, D. C.: Public Affairs Press, 1945), p. 45.

11. *Ibid.,* p. 69.

the committee chairmen and ranking majority members will tend
to be Southerners, and when the Republicans organize the Senate
or House, they will tend to represent Northern rural areas. This
phenomenon has long been noted. Moreover, a few of the Democratic chairmen will be products of city machines, which can
guarantee reelection to the faithful party lieutenant. Many chairmen will speak for a dominant group interest at home; as long
as they do so they stay in office, no matter what their record on
other matters.

The seniority system stacks the cards against those areas where
competition for votes is the keenest, where the two-party system
is the liveliest, where political currents run fresh and free. It
stacks them in favor of the politically stagnant districts—those
made "safe" for the incumbent by the poll tax and other restrictions on voting, by the monopolistic position of one party, by the
ascendancy of a major interest group, by city or rural machines.
These states and districts are, of course, as deserving of representation in Congress as any other. But the system is rigged to
give them undue weight, and in general to put power in the hands
of those members of Congress least aware of the problems of
modern industrial society and least equipped to deal with them.

For many years there has been clamor for the reform of a
system which, in Roland Young's words, flouts "established political principles: that of party government; of a legislature responsible to the electoral mandate; and of the utilization of the
best material for the most important offices."[12] Progress has been
scant. While the congressional reorganization act took a little
discretion from chairmen by requiring them to report promptly
bills approved by their committees, it evaded the seniority issue
altogether. This omission was hardly surprising, for even the joint
committee drawing up reorganization proposals had been silent
on the matter. It was reported that its members failed to agree on
workable changes.

Actually there are several feasible alternatives. Chairmen

12. *This Is Congress* (New York: Alfred A. Knopf, 1943), pp. 108-109.

could be chosen by their committees, by the Speaker or majority leaders, by party caucus, or the job could rotate automatically among the committee majority. Indeed, at least two of these methods have been used in the House when the automatic workings of seniority would have produced an intolerable situation.[13] But exceptions to the seniority rule are rare. In 1941, for instance, Senator Robert R. Reynolds of North Carolina, an isolationist, became chairman of the Committee on Military Affairs at the height of the defense effort; there was widespread protest inside and outside Congress but nothing could be done.

If precedents exist for bypassing the seniority system, if workable alternatives are at hand, how explain its tenacious grip over congressional machinery? The usual defense of the system is that it favors the "more experienced" legislators. Experience may or may not bring wisdom, but even if it does, the seniority rule is self-contradictory. For that rule advances only those members of Congress with the longest continuous service; if a highly experienced member drops out of Congress for a time, he sacrifices any seniority he accumulated on his committees.

Senator Sherman of Ohio, chairman of the Finance committee, left the Senate in 1877 to serve as Secretary of the Treasury under Hayes; when he returned to the Senate four years later he became the lowest-ranking member of that committee, although he was clearly the most experienced. Similarly, Joseph G. Cannon, who during his 38 years in the House had served for a long time at the top of the Appropriations committee, had to start all over again at the bottom after skipping a term as the result of his defeat in 1912.

The real reason that Congress tolerates seniority is its incapacity to organize itself as an effective tool of representative democracy. Many years ago Speaker Reed noted scornfully that the majority seemed to be afraid of itself.[14] It still is. A few members

13. For variations in the rule see W. F. Willoughby, *Principles of Legislative Organization and Administration* (Washington: The Brookings Institution, 1934), pp. 352-354.

14. D. S. Alexander, *History and Procedure of the House of Representatives* (Boston: Houghton Mifflin Co., 1916), p. vi.

of Congress benefit from the rule and would fight for it; many others oppose it but they are divided and leaderless. Still others—and they hold the balance of power—acquiesce in the system because it tends to dull the impact of controversial issues on agreeable relationships within the two houses. Promotion by seniority, former Congressman Robert Luce once said, "conduces most to contentment and least endangers morale."[15] So it does, but only at the expense of democratic and efficient action.

THE OBSTRUCTIONISTS

THAT a handful of men can deadlock our legislative machinery is one of the marvels of American government. But considering the power of minority groups in Congress, it is hardly surprising that the filibuster and other devices, buttressed by elaborate parliamentary rules, are still used to obstruct the majority. For those devices are the logical extension—although to a new height of absurdity—of the instruments of minority control described herein.

The filibuster is a handy weapon for obstructionists in the Senate. At least as old as the Constitution, it has become part of the political saga of America. One thinks of Huey Long, hoarse and disheveled, holding the Senate floor for fifteen and one-half hours in 1935 as he quoted the Bible, lectured on the Constitution, and offered recipes for fried oysters and pot-likker, Louisiana-style. Or of "Fighting Bob" La Follette's filibuster of eighteen hours against the Aldrich-Vreeland currency bill in 1908—a record for continuous holding of the Senate floor, although the Wisconsin progressive husbanded his strength by means of quorum calls and other interruptions. Or of Senator John T. Morgan of Alabama, who, although nearing his eightieth year, was able almost single-handed to hold up ratification of the Colombian treaty for the Panama canal (the Senator wanted a canal through Nicaragua) and to force President Theodore Roosevelt

15. Robert Luce, *Congress: An Explanation* (Cambridge: Harvard University Press, 1926), p. 9.

to convene the Senate in special session to gain approval of the treaty.

Far more serious even than the one-man filibuster is the organized, cooperative filibuster staged by a determined group of Senators. Spelling one another day after day, often catching their opponents off guard with parliamentary stratagems, and showing a hardihood usually not matched by the unorganized majority, such obstructionists can hold up the Senate for weeks at a time.

It was this kind of filibuster, conducted by no more than a dozen Senators, that balked passage of the Armed Ship Bill in 1917 and drew from President Wilson an angry attack on the "little group of wilful men" who had "rendered the great Government of the United States helpless and contemptible."

It is this kind of filibuster that Southerners have used on several occasions to kill anti-lynching bills; one of these, in 1937-38, held up Senate business for six weeks. Sometimes group obstructionism is hard to detect, for it may take the form of a general slowdown of Senate machinery rather than outright sabotage. Sometimes the participants publicize and dramatize their battle in order to attain heroic proportions in the eyes of their constituents. The filibuster is so effective a weapon for obstructionists that often their mere threat to use it is sufficient to gain their purposes.[16]

Inevitably there has been sharp protest against a system that amounts to a *reductio ad absurdum* of the idea of minority rights, that "denies two premises of the democratic process: the ability of reason to persuade; and the ability of the majority to act."[17] Scholars have persistently argued that there is a profound difference between the minority's right to delay measures long enough to focus public attention on them, and its ability to delay measures for weeks and defeat them altogether. Both political parties have gone on record against such obstructionism.

16. For a history of the filibuster, see F. L. Burdette, *Filibustering in the Senate* (Princeton: Princeton University Press, 1940).

17. Young, *op. cit.*, p. 145.

Vice-President Charles G. Dawes conducted a crusade against a system which he felt could not but "lessen the effectiveness, prestige, and dignity of the United States Senate."

"The remedy?" asked President Wilson following the Armed Ship Bill filibuster. "There is but one remedy. The only remedy is that the rules of the Senate shall be so altered that it can act."

Shortly thereafter, on March 8, 1917, the Senate adopted the cloture rule. Under its terms the upper chamber by a two-thirds vote can halt debate. This form of cloture, mild as it is, had been invoked only four times out of twenty-five attempts up through 1948. Not since 1927 has debate been cut off under the rule.

If cloture by two-thirds vote is ineffective against a determined filibuster, why has not the Senate adopted cloture by simple majority? One reason is the confusion within the Senate—and outside of it—over the proper scope of minority rights. The chief reason is the reluctance of most Senators to weaken a tool for obstruction that they themselves may need to employ some day. "There are tacit understandings in the Senate," Burdette says, "bearing a close resemblance to 'log-rolling,' by virtue of which minority elements often combine against cloture even if only a few are strongly opposed to the measure upon which it is moved."[18]

Underlying this fact is a strange fear of majority rule. Senator Henry Cabot Lodge contended in 1893 that "there is another right more sacred in a legislative body than the right of debate, and that is the right to vote." Senator Henry Moore Teller replied next day, "There is nothing in the world more wicked and cruel than the majority; and governments are instituted and preserved to protect minorities against majorities."

Teller's protest has echoed down the years in the upper chamber, not least in the words of Senator Tydings of Maryland during a filibuster in 1946: "The rule of majority, the rule of votes. Majority to hades...." Obstructionists fear that the majority may

18. *Op. cit.*, p. 222.

be irresponsible, forgetting that the minority can be irresponsible, too.

The tenacity of this minority tradition was dramatized once again in the filibuster of March, 1949. Rallying against President Truman's civil rights program, Southerners argued that cloture could be invoked only against bills—not against motions to discuss bills. Although such an interpretation made cloture almost useless, the Southerners gained enough backing from Republicans and a few Northern Democrats to thwart an attempt by the Administration to establish a broader interpretation.

Having won the day, the Southerners and their allies arranged a "compromise" rule. Under the new formula cloture may be applied against any motion or measure—except a change in Senate rules—but only if voted by two-thirds of the whole Senate membership (64 out of 96) rather than by two-thirds of the Senators on the floor. Since a dozen Senators are normally absent from the floor, the actual result of the change is to strengthen the veto power of a handful of Senators defending the Solid South or any other region or interest. The new rule was not a compromise but a harsh peace imposed by the defenders of minority rule.

There are other weapons in the obstructionists' arsenal besides the filibuster, although no other so important. Interminable points of order and appeals to the chair, dilatory motions, introducing irrelevant business, and frequent quorum calls are some of the methods used in the House as well as the Senate. Often these devices are employed in conjunction with a filibuster in the upper house.

Studying the attempts during 1941-1946 to set up a statutory Fair Employment Practice Commission and to preserve the President's Committee on Fair Employment Practice, Will Maslow found that the "resourceful parliamentarians on both sides of the issue have utilized such devices as points of order, discharge petitions, Calendar Wednesdays, blocking the appointment of conference committees, restrictions in appropriation acts, suspension of the rules, special orders of business, and breaking quorums."[19] There is no sign that the practices of obstruction are decreasing.

THE CONSEQUENCES

THE total effect of unfair districting, unrepresentative committees, the seniority rule, and obstructionism in Congress is fourfold:

(1) They prevent Congress from reflecting more fairly the sentiment of the people as a whole. In general the rural population and producer interests are over-represented, urban groups and consumer interests are under-represented.

(2) They often stop Congress from acting at all. The filibuster, although it can be used to gain support for some measure, is essentially a negative instrument, a means of blocking action. So is the power of the committee chairman: he can frustrate action by his fellow committee members, but he cannot so easily expedite a measure.

(3) They weaken Congress further as an instrument of majority rule. Blocs representing localities, sections, and special interests take advantage of the organization and rules of each house to hamstring the disorganized, undisciplined majority.

(4) They intensify the problem of the separation of powers between executive and legislative branches. As a result of these factors Congress speaks for a different constellation of forces than does the President. Congress often evades the supreme job of democratic government, which is the adjustment of differences among groups in order to find the basis for joint action by at least a majority. Nor does it feel impelled to go along with the programs of president or party.

There are, of course, means of offsetting in Congress the divisive, negative forces described above. The tools for majority action have received slight treatment in this chapter because they

19. "FEPC—A Case History in Parliamentary Maneuver," *The University of Chicago Law Review,* June 1946, Vol. XIII, No. 4, p. 407.

largely are unavailing against the minorities. The Speaker of the House was once a powerful force for promoting majority rule, but his wings were clipped in the revolts of 1911-1913. The caucus has a humble role in either house. The majority leaders are influential, but more in the realm of procedure than in that of policy. This is not to say that the speaker, caucus, majority leaders, and whips could not be converted into powerful weapons for majority rule. They could be so converted almost over night. What is lacking is the will on the part of most members of Congress to sweep the devices for minority rule out of both their houses and to make Congress more responsible to a majority of the voters.

V

```
ЛЛЛЛЛЛЛЛЛЛЛЛЛЛЛЛЛЛЛЛЛЛЛЛ
```

The Story of Three Bills

FROM the beginning Congress has often served as a cockpit for bouts between rival interests. The initial measure introduced in the very first session of Congress in 1789 was a tariff bill. The representatives of various sections were alert, and soon they were sparring for local advantage.

"Pennsylvania wanted a tariff on molasses, rum and especially steel. Massachusetts agreed upon the latter but was dubious of the others since they constituted important items in her carrying trade. Southerners opposed a tariff on steel, and western opposition to the tax on salt was overcome by providing a tariff on hemp."[1]

Today the battles over vitally important economic legislation —taxation, spending, wages, public works, prices, employment, currency, finance, and others—are fought out on basically the same terms as in 1789. To track a bill through House and Senate is to unfold a panorama of Congress in action. The following accounts of three bills show:

The way in which pressure groups operate in Congress to block, promote, or cripple legislation.

The corrosive effect of localism on legislative action.

1. P. H. Odegard and E. A. Helms, *American Politics,* 2nd ed. (New York: Harper & Brothers, 1947), p. 31.

The limited function of political parties in Congressional policy-making.

The vital role of the President in drawing up measures and confronting Congress with them, and in mediating among the organized minorities.

The effect on legislation of the committee system and the seniority rule.

The devices used by Congressmen to straddle issues and to conceal their position.

These measures—the Fair Labor Standards Act of 1938, the Emergency Price Control Act of 1942, and the Missouri Valley Authority Bill—typify the manner in which Congress has made economic policies since the close of Franklin D. Roosevelt's brief honeymoon with the legislative branch. The extensions of price control and its final dismantling in Congress, for example, had many of the characteristics of the original enactment. In the struggle over the St. Lawrence Seaway proposals, as in that over MVA, Senators have acted primarily in terms of the immediate effect of the project on their states rather than on the basis of its benefits to the whole nation. Efforts to raise minimum wage standards have led to deadlocks reminiscent of the more spectacular handling of the wages and hours bill in 1937-38. In these and many other cases the details vary from bill to bill and from year to year, but the pattern remains the same.

WAGES AND HOURS: ACT ONE

VIEWING the American political scene early in 1937, one might have assumed that no bill would have an easier journey through Congress than one seeking to shorten the working day and to abolish starvation wages. This reform, which had been in effect in other countries for years, was long overdue in the United States. Following the 1936 elections the political setting seemed ideal for quick action by President and Congress. Both party platforms had made pious gestures toward the need for improved wage and hour standards. Candidate Roosevelt had proclaimed that he "had only just begun to fight" for improved working conditions, and in forty-six states the voters had endorsed his stand. His party dominated Congress, holding nearly four-fifths of the seats in each chamber. Opposition strength was so low that only two Republicans were on the 13-man Committee on Education and Labor in the Senate.

As it turned out, the Fair Labor Standards Act emerged only after a stormy twelve-month period of gestation. Surviving a series of near-miscarriages and attempted abortions during three separate sessions of Congress, the infant bill finally appeared, crippled, undersized, and hardly recognizable to its progenitors.

Part of the trouble lay in a political miscalculation made by President Roosevelt himself. Originally he had planned to submit wages and hours legislation to Congress early in 1937. His assistants, Benjamin Cohen and Thomas Corcoran, redrafted a bill that had been prepared in the Department of Labor and took it to Senator Black, chairman of the Senate Committee on Education and Labor. Black agreed to sponsor the measure in the Senate. But in February 1937 the President suddenly announced his ill-fated court reform plan, and he later decided to postpone action on wages and hours on the mistaken assumption that the latter would be highly popular in Congress and would unify Democrats divided over court reform. He also believed, quite rightly, that some Roosevelt appointments were needed on the Supreme Court if an effective wages and hours act was to survive judicial scrutiny. The President's political tactic failed: Corcoran had to trade c.i the basis of both bills, and instead of helping to force through the court plan, the wages and hours bill was almost dragged down to defeat with it.

Black introduced the proposed Fair Labor Standards Act in the Senate on May 24, 1937, and Representative Connery of Massachusetts, chairman of the House Labor Committee, submitted a companion bill in the lower chamber. In a vigorous message to Congress on the same day the President urged congressional support for the measure. "We have promised it," he said. "We cannot stand still."

The bill combined the ideas of the Labor Department, Cohen and Corcoran, Black, and various labor leaders. Under its provisions a Fair Labor Standards Board of five members was to administer the act. Congress was to set statutory minimum wages and maximum hours, but the Board would have power to raise these standards. The bill was made highly flexible to meet the arguments of those who feared the sudden imposition of a wage strait jacket. Child labor was illegalized. Leon Henderson estimated that three million persons would enjoy higher labor standards under the measure.

On Roosevelt's suggestion, the Senate and House labor committees held joint hearings on the bill in order to speed action. Representatives of the National Association of Manufacturers, the United States Chamber of Commerce, the National Association of Wool Manufacturers, the Cotton Textile Institute, and the Anthracite Institute appeared before the committees to contend against the proposed act.

Individual businessmen did not, however, present such a common front. They tended to divide along sectional lines, Northern businessmen supporting the bill as a means of offsetting low-wage competition in the South and Southern businessmen opposing it. Representatives of many farm and agricultural processing groups appeared to request exemption from the terms of the legislation.

Differences among the factions of organized labor were greater than those among businessmen. Both William Green, chief of the American Federation of Labor, and John L. Lewis, then chairman of the Committee for Industrial Organization, generally favored the bill but they had major reservations. Green feared that governmental regulation of wages and hours might weaken the AFL by interfering with collective bargaining. Lewis opposed governmental fixing of wages at any rate above 40 cents an hour on the grounds that the government rate might become a fixed wage.

It was clear that both Green and Lewis were concerned with rights of union labor rather than with the needs of the millions of unorganized workers who had no unions to lean on. On the other hand, Sidney Hillman, representing the Amalgamated Clothing Workers of America, did not share the fears of the other two labor leaders, for he dealt with a "low-standard" industry where collective bargaining could not cover the whole industry, thus requiring governmental intervention if conditions were to be improved uniformly. These labor views, especially Green's, were to prove fateful in the history of the wages and hours act.

Following the hearings, the Senate Committee on Education and Labor proceeded to revise the bill extensively, completing its work early in July. The chief effect of the committee amendments was to curb drastically the powers of the proposed board, which now could not fix wages at a rate over 40 cents an hour or a standard work week at less than 40 hours. Instead of setting up statutory minimum wages or maximum hours, however, the Senate committee left this power to the board. Child labor standards were lowered to permit children under 16 to work in jobs not injuring their health or interfering with their schooling. Dozens of exemptions were written into the measure—local retailing, railroad employees, forestry, farming, dairying, fishing, and others.

Just why the committee modified the bill so drastically is not wholly clear. President Roosevelt had stated at a press conference in June that he would not welcome attempts to change the provisions of the Black-Connery bill. His remarks indicated, however, that he was not opposed to amendments for their own sake but because they might endanger passage of the bill. Actually, the President was not interested in the details of the bill; he wanted mainly to enlist wide support for it and push it through. Some committee members, it is clear, were willing to make concessions to gain necessary support for the measure. At any rate, the bill as revised received unanimous support in the Committee on Education and Labor, everyone present, including one Republican, voting to report it favorably.

Already opposition to the bill was mounting among influential groups in the South. Postmaster General Farley reported to the President that key Democratic officials in Alabama and Mississippi had been induced to attack the bill.[2] Senator Harrison of Mississippi came out against the bill; the fact that he lost out on July 21 to Senator Barkley for the position of majority leader of the upper chamber, with the Administration quietly supporting the Kentucky New Dealer, dramatized the division within the Democratic party. Black was under heavy attack in Alabama for his sponsorship of the measure.

But the worst threat to the bill was taking shape within the top councils of the American Federation of Labor. William Hutcheson of the building trades, John Frey of the metal trades, and other powerful AFL officials feared that the wages and hours bill might interfere with existing arrangements protecting their crafts. Lewis and Green wanted a wages and hours bill, but their position on the version before the Senate was ambiguous. Members of the Senate labor bloc refused to commit themselves on the bill until they knew the AFL's position. What was the Federation's stand? Frantic telephone calls only partly cleared up the matter.

"All in all," remarked *The New York Times,* "that was a stimulating and inspiring sight over the week end at Washington as members of the United States Senate brought to bear all their powers of analysis and intuition on the crucial question of what does Mr. Green really think, what does Mr. Frey really think, and what does Mr. Lewis really think."[3]

The wages and hours bill came within seven votes of being defeated when the motion to recommit was lost by a vote of 36-48. After that the frontal attack on the bill in the Senate was not

2. File 2730, Franklin D. Roosevelt Library, Hyde Park, N. Y.
3. August 2, 1937, p. 18.

severe. Senatorial factions were able, however, to obtain exemptions of "marginal activities" from the bill. Seasonal industries, such as canning, were freed from the hours restrictions. An effort of a Republican-Southern Democrat coalition to exempt tobacco warehouses, cotton compresses, cotton ginning and baling, and cotton warehouses from the wage and hour regulations lost only by a tie vote, 40-40. On July 31, 1937, by a vote of 56-28, the Senate passed the bill. Thirteen Republican Senators voted against the measure, along with 15 Democrats, eight of whom were Southerners.

President Roosevelt realized that even this weaker version of wages and hours legislation would fail unless he could induce the AFL to support it wholeheartedly. It was clear that the House Labor Committee would not dare withstand the Federation. Accordingly the President summoned Green to a peace parley. The AFL head asked for amendments to prevent the proposed board from interfering in areas of successful collective bargaining, or from interfering with the operations of the Walsh-Healey Act (which maintained labor standards on government supply contracts), or from establishing minimum wages lower than the prevailing wage. Roosevelt felt that these concessions could be made without hurting the bill. In his own hand he wrote to Mrs. Mary Norton, who had become chairman of the House Labor Committee upon Connery's death in June:[4]

> O.K. on Green's suggestions:
> (1) Not below going wage in vicinity
> (2) Not hurt collective bargaining
> (3) Not hurt Walsh-Healey bill.

With Green's blessing the bill and his amendments were speedily endorsed by the House Labor Committee by August 6. To placate the Southerners, a new committee amendment provided that two of the five board members would be appointed from the South. But Southern Democrats in the House were not mollified. They had an effective weapon handy in the Rules Committee, on which five of their number—Dies of Texas, Smith of

4. File 2730, Franklin D. Roosevelt Library, Hyde Park, N. Y.

Virginia, Cox of Georgia, Driver of Arkansas, and Clark of North Carolina—held the balance of power between northern Democrats and Republicans. Only the Rules Committee could give the wages and hours bill right of way on the House floor, and the Southerners and the Republicans on the committee refused to grant the necessary rule. The reason, they explained, was that the bill had not received sufficient consideration.

In vain did a group of liberal Representatives try to force a Democratic caucus to press for action on the bill. The 157 Democrats who showed up failed by eight votes to become an official caucus; a score of others were nearby in the cloakroom but failed to answer their names, provoking an attack by John L. Lewis on members of Congress "skulking in hallways and closets" to prevent a quorum. Helpless to take further action on the bill, Congress adjourned. Wrote a *New York Times* correspondent: "The history of the Wages and Hours Bill is ... that of the triumph of a minority."[5]

WAGES AND HOURS: ACT TWO

PRESIDENT ROOSEVELT refused to abandon the fight for an effective wages and hours bill. Even before the first session of the 75th Congress had run its course, he was thinking of calling a special session in the fall to take up wages and hours and other "must" legislation. In mid-October he summoned Congress to convene on November 15. Meanwhile he pressed the wage-hour issue on several fronts. He conferred on parliamentary strategy with House Majority Leader McCormack, who believed that a discharge petition could be used to pry the bill out of the Rules Committee. Chairman O'Connor of the Rules Committee, probably at the suggestion of Mr. Roosevelt, wrote each member of the committee urging that the House be allowed to vote on the legislation. The Chief Executive kept the issue before the people in radio talks.

5. August 22, 1937, IV, p. 3.

Despite these efforts, it became apparent soon after Congress convened that the Republican-Southern Democrat coalition on the Rules Committee would not release the bill. This development proved the hollowness of their previous excuse that more consideration was needed; it was also the signal for Mrs. Norton, in behalf of the Labor Committee, to file a petition to discharge the Rules Committee. A drive for the necessary 218 signatures was begun. Over 100 Representatives quickly signed, but then the pace slowed almost to a halt.

With the support of the President, backers of wages and hours legislation used every available method to gain signatures, including various "trades" on the basis of other legislation or favors. When Marvin Jones of Texas, chairman of the House Agriculture Committee, added his name, it seemed likely that a deal had been made involving support of wages and hours by the farm bloc in exchange for votes for an important agricultural bill by labor representatives. Slowly the list of signatures grew. "They have swapped everything today but the Capitol," Dies protested, and Representative Hamilton Fish of New York demanded an investigation of lobbying by the Administration. On December 2 the necessary 218 signatures—a majority of the House—were gained. Only nine Republicans, however, and not one representative of four Southern states, signed the petition.

The bill overcame this hurdle only to run into another. In October the AFL in convention had repudiated even Green's lukewarm endorsement of the wages and hours bill. He was instructed to take no action on wages and hours legislation without conferring first with Hutcheson, Frey, and the other members of the Federation's executive council. The House Labor Committee tried to meet AFL objections by writing a new bill under which an administrator in the Labor Department wielding limited power would administer the act, rather than a board enjoying some discretion.

This effort of the House Labor Committee to satisfy the AFL proved a complete failure. On December 3, the day after the battle over the discharge petition had been won, Green came out for a wholly different approach. He now favored a bill providing simply for a 40-cent minimum and a 40-hour maximum, with an eight-hour day. Since the administration of such inflexible provisions would involve no discretion, Green's bill would have had federal district attorneys enforce these standards by means of criminal proceedings. Green could hardly have expected favorable action on this bill. It ran counter to the ideas of the Administration, the Senate, and the House Labor Committee. It reflected AFL opposition to any effective wages and hours legislation.

There now ensued a battle between two bills. Mrs. Norton and the House leadership planned to take the initiative in forcing the new Labor Committee bill to a record vote before the AFL version and other threatening amendments could be brought onto the floor. This strategy misfired, however, when Representatives acting for the AFL used a parliamentary maneuver to gain priority for consideration of their bill.

Bitter debate followed. So many warring factions were now involved that unity on any one proposal seemed impossible. Action was slowed by an almost endless series of procedural snarls. Meanwhile, opponents of any and all wage-hour bills sat back in satisfaction, knowing that they could throw their strength in such a way as to defeat the bills.

Such was the fate of the two measures. AFL Congressmen were so hostile to the committee version that Representative Connery of Massachusetts, brother of the late Labor Committee chairman and as loyal a supporter of the Federation, demanded that the family name be taken out of the Black-Connery bill, leaving it simply as the "Black bill." On December 15 the AFL bill was rejected, 162-131. Immediately Green telegraphed every Representative asking that the committee bill be recommitted.

The Federation's lobbyists buttonholed Representatives in the corridors. During the sharp debate that followed, member after member took advantage of the labor split to gain exemptions for workers engaged in industries in their own districts. So many of these attempts were successful that Dies sardonically introduced an amendment that read:

Within 90 days after appointment of the Administrator, she shall report to Congress whether anyone in the United States is subject to this bill . . .

In vain Mrs. Norton tried to enlist support from the farm bloc for the committee bill. Every Democratic member of the House Labor Committee but one had supported the farm bill to show their good faith. But the farm bloc did not reciprocate. Powerful agricultural organizations, such as the National Grange and the National Cooperative Milk Producers' Federation, were fighting the bill because they feared it would increase farm labor costs and industrial prices.

Aroused by reports of a campaign to stir up farmers against the bill, President Roosevelt asked the Justice Department to find out who was paying for it; the FBI reported that the Southern Pine Association was one of the financing groups.[6]

On December 17 the House voted to recommit the wages and hours bill by a vote of 216-198. Of the 133 Democrats opposing the legislation, over half were from the South. Probably the Southern opposition would have been greater had not cotton ginning and cotton storage been exempted from the bill. In a bitter speech analyzing the reason for the defeat, Representative John A. Martin of Colorado put his finger on the basic deception involved:

What the labor split did was to furnish an alibi, an escapement, for many Members not favorable to such legislation, but who would not have dared to vote against it on the final roll call. They can now go back to their districts and, availing themselves of the Green letters and telegrams, say they were for a "real" wage-hour bill, but not the "abortion" before the House, and get away with it. There will be political casualties growing out of the death of

6. Correspondence, File 2730, Franklin D. Roosevelt Library, Hyde Park, N. Y.

the wage-hour bill, and perhaps as many among its friends as among its enemies. Such is the game.

WAGES AND HOURS: ACT THREE

THERE were some who gave up hope that Congress ever could produce a wage-hour bill. It seemed that any such legislation inevitably would be ground to pieces between two mighty forces in Congress—the Southern Democrats and the AFL bloc. But the President and the liberals in Congress decided to carry the fight into the 1938 session of Congress.

Mr. Roosevelt was highly displeased over the Southern desertions, but willing to make concessions. Although he did not favor North-South wage differentials he would cede such a clause to the Southerners in return for their support. He urged the farm bloc to support labor legislation in return for help that labor representatives had given on farm measures. And he sounded out the AFL on its minimum demands.

The Chief Executive would not go too far. When Representative Dies proposed a wage-hour bill that would permit states to set lower standards than those to be provided under the national law and that would give a privileged position to the oil industry, the Texan met head-on resistance. "Call up Martin Dies," Mr. Roosevelt instructed his secretary, Marvin McIntyre, after studying the proposal, "and tell him that any idea of having an individual State vary a national Wages and Hours bill is not only unsound, but would destroy the effectiveness of building up a purchasing power in those sections most needing it, and the President regards it as the weakest, most dangerous proposition he has ever heard. Tell him further that if we start to legislate for the oil industry, we'll be aiding and abetting those people who want to exempt the canners, the cheese factories, and the lumber mills, and that that is completely unsound."[7]

The President told visitors on another occasion that low-wage

7. File 2730, Franklin D. Roosevelt Library, Hyde Park, N. Y.

districts were fighting wage-hour legislation: "Whenever you start to get a wages and hours bill, the Congressman for that particular district gets a piteous plea, 'For God's sake don't do anything or you won't go back to Congress.' So, he tries to get an amendment to take care of his district. That is pure selfishness."

The ticklish job of finding a mutually acceptable formula went on during the first quarter of 1938. On the basis of drafts prepared by Gerard D. Reilly of the Labor Department, the Administration decided on a new version that would create a division of wages and hours under an administrator who would appoint tripartite boards to investigate, hold hearings, and recommend wage-hour standards within the limitations of 40 cents per hour and 40 hours per week. The President added to this draft a North-South differential as bait to win over the South.

The AFL chiefs continued to hold out. They were still hostile to a federal board or administrator with broad powers and they did not want North-South differentials. They would accept only the AFL version that had been defeated in the House in December. With the President's backing Mrs. Norton appointed a subcommittee under Representative Ramspeck of Georgia to work out a new Labor Committee draft acceptable to all groups. Mr. Roosevelt invited Green and several of the craft leaders to the White House and gained a promise from them that they would support "a bill."

The Ramspeck subcommittee measure was now ready. Resembling somewhat the original Senate bill, it would have set up a five-man board with power to fix minimum wages and maximum hours within the old 40-40 limit and would have made possible regional differentials. But when Green saw this version, he turned it down and asked the House Labor Committee to do likewise. The committee dutifully undertook to write a new version that would satisfy the Federation.

By April 13 the committee had finished its new draft which, it hoped, would receive Green's blessing. This draft was somewhat similar to the AFL bill that had failed in December: the administration of the act was under the Secretary of Labor; flat standards that might be changed from year to year were set up in the bill; and no geographical differentials were provided for. Green and his colleagues still did not fully agree with this bill. But now they were under pressure both from the Administration and from the rank and file. Furthermore, the CIO was campaigning for a wage-hour bill, and the AFL did not want to be outflanked on an important piece of labor legislation. So Green gave this bill his reluctant support.

The House Labor Committee now had to choose between two bills: one backed by the Federation and by most of the labor bloc in the Committee and in the House, the other (the Ramspeck draft) by the Administration and by some of the Southern Democrats. The committee was bound to make enemies whichever way it voted. In this awkward situation the members were disposed to stall. The President was pressing for a decision, but when Mrs. Norton convened the Labor Committee, the members met, debated, and adjourned without action.

By this time another Administration aide, Rufus G. Poole, had become a leading actor in the legislative drama. An old hand at Congressional matters, Poole was transferred to the Labor Department from the Interior Department for the express purpose of managing the wage-hour legislation. Although he and Benjamin Cohen had assisted in drafting the Ramspeck subcommittee proposal, Poole, like the President, was willing to accept any bill provided it was reasonably effective. Poole made an elaborate canvass of the House to determine precisely how members felt about wages and hours legislation.

As a result of his investigation Poole became convinced that the only way to break the deadlock was for the Administration to support the AFL draft and then seek to improve it in conference. This became the plan of action. At a Labor Committee meeting on April 14 Ramspeck argued for his draft, but he was defeated in committee by two votes. Poole then advised Mrs. Norton to entertain a motion for the AFL bill. Some of the members wished to adjourn, pleading that they needed more time to consider this draft, but Mrs. Norton managed to hold them in session. Late in the afternoon the committee reported out the AFL version by a 14-4 vote.

The next hurdle was the Rules Committee. Since the Labor Committee bill lacked a wage differential, however, the Southerners on the Rules Committee were as adamant as ever. Once again it would be necessary to use the discharge petition.

The Administration's strategy was to delay the petition until the results of the May senatorial primary in Florida became known. Political experts in the Administration knew that Pepper would win. Poole reasoned that if Pepper could be induced to speak vigorously for the wage-hour bill during his campaign, his victory would be interpreted as a test of sentiment on the bill in the South. Over $10,000 was turned over to the Pepper campaign fund by Corcoran, who had obtained the sum from a radio corporation executive on the basis of another deal. Coincident with these negotiations a nation-wide drive was launched in support of the legislation. All labor groups rallied behind the bill, and the backing of Northern business groups was solicited.

On May 3 Pepper won a decisive primary victory in Florida. When the discharge petition was opened for signature in the House three days later, the necessary 218 signatures were gained in less than two and one-half hours. Some Representatives were vexed to find that they had appeared too late to sign the "honor roll." On May 24, after a tumultuous session lasting nearly twelve hours, the House passed the Labor Committee bill by a vote of 314-97.

The Senate and the House bills now differed so radically that the conference committee would have to act virtually as a third house of Congress to harmonize them. Consequently, every faction wished to have its representatives on the conference committee. The Southerners and the AFL bloc were as mulish as ever. Green threatened to call for the defeat of the measure if the Senate version remained, and 17 Southern Senators resolved to filibuster unless differentials were retained. The 14-man conference committee, representing a wide range of interests, labored for two weeks amid charges and countercharges aired throughout the country. It was necessary to pledge the members to secrecy on the nature of the deliberations because pressure groups were so active.

On June 11, the committee reached agreement. The final version set up a single administrator in the Labor Department. The 40-cent wage minimum and the 40-hour maximum would be reached after a two-year transition period. Industry advisory committees were provided for, and a number of exemptions were written in. The question of differentials was in effect left to the administrators of the act.

The long drama was almost over. On June 14 both the House and the Senate accepted the conference report, without major opposition. Signing the act on June 25, 1938, the President exclaimed, with a sigh of relief, "That's that."

PRICE CONTROL—OR FARM RELIEF?

NO GREAT industrial nation can fight a modern war without some kind of price control, for heavy spending and short supplies form an explosive inflationary mixture. But if the pressure politicians in Congress had had their way, the United States would have entered World War II with a feeble price control program that could not possibly have coped with the tremendous pressures toward inflation.

President Roosevelt took initial steps toward stabilization in 1940 and early 1941 by placing Leon Henderson in charge of presidential agencies that had broad jurisdiction over prices but no real power to enforce decisions. Early in 1941 Henderson and his legal advisor, David Ginsburg, advised the President that it was time to seek congressional action to bolster price control, but it was not until July of that year that the President considered the political climate suitable for requesting a drastic grant of power from the legislators.

President Roosevelt sent a message to Congress on July 30, 1941, urging a comprehensive price control act for the sake of the "general welfare." His action came none too soon. One corporation had already brushed aside a Henderson order, and inflationary pressures were mounting.

Henderson and Ginsburg had been drafting price control legislation since December 1940. They were in the unique position of being able to provide in their drafts for the day-to-day problems they were meeting on the job. Perhaps the thorniest issue they faced was whether or not the proposed congressional act should provide for wage stabilization as well as price control.

Bernard Baruch was campaigning for an integrated program that would cope with wages as well as prices. Henderson and Ginsburg decided, however, that wages should be left to another agency. The President concurred. Knowing the strength of the labor and farm blocs in Congress, he feared that an act combining both wage and price control would never survive Senate and House action.

Vice-President Henry Wallace, at Mr. Roosevelt's suggestion, was enlisted to help push the bill through Congress. He set up a committee of Senators, Representatives, and Administration officials to plan strategy and to revise the final Administration price control draft in the light of Congressional attitudes. Already members of the farm bloc, both Republicans and Democrats, were assailing proposals to freeze farm prices. To meet such objections the Wallace committee wrote in a section providing that ceilings for agricultural commodities could not be set at lower than 100 per cent of parity. Other provisions in the Administration draft, such as the rent section, were modified. President Roosevelt endorsed the new bill.

The parliamentary strategy of the Wallace committee was to submit the bill first to the House, so that whatever damage was done to the bill in the lower chamber could be repaired in the Senate, where the President had powerful adherents in such Senators as Barkley and Wagner. This decision put the chairman of the House Committee on Banking and Currency, Representative Henry B. Steagall of Alabama, in a crucial role, for his would be the first legislative group to consider the bill. Steagall was not anti-Administration, but he represented a cotton district and he was under great pressure from agricultural organizations generally.

Steagall lost little time exploiting his opportunity. Discussing the bill with Ginsburg one day, he suddenly pulled from his pocket a clause providing that farm prices could not be set at less than 110 per cent of parity. Ginsburg demurred, stating that such a provision would upset the stabilization program. Steagall made it clear, however, that if the Administration rejected his clause he would allow price control to be gutted in committee. Knowing the destructive power of a hostile committee chairman, the Administration capitulated. A new Administration draft contained Steagall's clause.

Steagall introduced the price control bill in the House on August 1, 1941, and hearings before the Banking and Currency Committee got under way five days later. Rarely has legislation received such extended consideration at the hands of a House committee as did the Emergency Price Control Act of 1942. The 37 sessions of the committee lasted over a three-month period, and the printed transcript ran to 2305 pages. Henderson was the first witness. For fifteen days he was subjected to hour-after-hour interrogation on all phases of the economic situation, as well as on his own political beliefs. He approved the 110 per cent of parity clause, but without enthusiasm.

The farm bloc held the balance of power on the committee. One of its members, Representative Paul Brown of Georgia, outdid even a farm lobbyist in his zeal for protecting agricultural interests. When President Edward A. O'Neal of the American Farm Bureau Federation testified in support of 110 per cent of parity, Brown stated that cotton growers should receive more than 110 per cent, only to be warned by O'Neal, "We do not want to shoot the works." Nevertheless, O'Neal opposed the bill because it lacked wage controls, and representatives of other farm organizations took a similar stand.

On November 1 the House Committee on Banking and Currency reported out an amended price control bill. The amendments testified to the strength of the farm bloc in the committee. Along with the 110 per cent of parity clause there were special pricing provisions that would have permitted sharp increases in farm prices. The committee also weakened the bill by cancelling the government's proposed licensing powers and its power to buy and sell commodities, both of which provisions were considered vital to an effective stabilization program.

The Administration greeted the amended bill with dismay. Government economists estimated that the new provisions would allow farm prices to rise 20 per cent over the 110 per cent of parity level. Steagall himself admitted that the bill would not "control inflation completely."

The price control bill faced an exceptionally potent coalition made up of a large portion of the Republicans in the House, most of the farm bloc, a group of Southern Democrats opposed to enhanced presidential powers, and representatives of various special interests that had a stake in rising commodity prices. Farm organizations were actively stirring up sentiment against a strong bill in the farm constituencies. Congressional leaders were plainly pessimistic over the chances of gaining a better bill from the committee, but the President and his aides pressed the issue.

President Roosevelt sent a vigorous note to Steagall, written by Henderson, asking at least that the licensing and buy-sell provisions be restored. By a feat of legerdemain the Administration was able to win back these two provisions from the committee on the eve of consideration by the full House. But how long could the recovered ground be held?

The Rules Committee displayed its pervasive influence over legislation by granting the price control bill a "wide open" rule which, unlike the usual rigid rules accorded important legislation, would permit organized minorities in the House to gain their various ends. "As one who is bitterly opposed to the bill as it has been presented by the Committee," declared Representative Fred L. Crawford of Michigan, "I want to congratulate . . . the Rules Committee for bringing in a broad, wide-open rule."[8]

Debate in the House was marked by acerbity among various elements of the majority party, charges against Henderson, and considerable confusion as to the need for and nature of price control. Majority leader McCormack warned the farm representatives not to tamper too much with the price control bill if they wished not to lose favorable votes on a soil conservation measure soon to come before the House.

There were the usual attempts to gain special advantages for particular economic groups. A Californian moved for the inclusion of grapes under the agricultural provisions, for example, and Steagall was successful in adding peanuts to the list of exempted commodities. Denouncing the bill because it did not sufficiently protect burley tobacco, Representative Edward W. Creal said: "I represent one of the largest burley-tobacco districts in America . . . If I come back here, it will be from the Fourth District of Kentucky, and as long as I am here, I am going to represent home folks first."[9]

The main reason for their opposition to the bill, members of the farm bloc proclaimed, was its failure to provide for wage controls. Given a chance to effect a thorough-going set of controls that would offer special favors to no group, would the farm bloc be willing to carry its share of the burden? The voting on the Gore amendment to the price control bill furnished an answer to this question.

Believing in the Baruch approach to stabilization, Representative Albert Gore of Tennessee for months had been trying to enlist support for a sweeping measure that would place ceilings on all wages, rents, and profits. Labor representatives had told him that they feared inflation but that they could not accept his pro-

8. *Congressional Record,* November 24, 1941, p. 9061.
9. *Ibid.,* November 28, 1941, p. 9234.

posals because of pressure "from below" against wage control. Farm Bureau Federation officials acclaimed the wage control provision, but said they would support the whole bill only if Gore accepted the 110 per cent of parity clause. Gore refused to make that concession. Lacking bloc support, his plan gained only five votes in the House Committee on Banking and Currency. On November 26 it met a similar fate in the House, with only 63 Representatives favoring it and 218 opposed. The defeat of Gore's amendment was conclusive proof that the farm and labor blocs in Congress would not, under these circumstances, yield their special demands for the sake of the general welfare. The defeat also seemed to justify President Roosevelt's strategy of submitting price control to Congress while undertaking wage stabilization on his own.

The price control bill that passed the House on November 28, 1941, by a vote of 224 to 161, was described as a "tattered remnant." The new measure embodied the crippling farm amendments, while in the closing hours of debate the House struck the licensing clause from the bill and weakened the buy-sell provision. Sixty-three Democrats, most of them Southerners, voted against the bill. The Administration's sole hope now was the Senate.

War came to the nation two days before the opening of hearings before the Senate Committee on Banking and Currency. In a wartime economy, Henderson told the committee, the House bill would be wholly unworkable, and he appealed for a "strong" bill. Shifting from his previous stand, he now supported a 100 per cent of parity clause, to the disgust of O'Neal, who reminded him that the President himself had accepted 110 per cent of parity.

On January 2, 1942, the Senate committee unanimously approved a bill that represented a notable victory for the Administration. A single price administrator, rather than the board provided for in the House bill, was given power to set selective ceilings. The licensing power was restored. The committee even modified the farm bloc amendments, although the 110 per cent of parity provision remained. Could the new bill withstand the powerful farm bloc in the Senate?

This question was not long in doubt. Perhaps not since the Smoot-Hawley tariff of 1930 had Congress been the scene of such bold and naked log-rolling as in the consideration of price control, when blocs and individual Senators reduced action on price control to the lowest terms of sectional and local advantage. Indeed, the tariff affair was the less serious, for that was a case of a congressional majority dividing up the spoils, while here a minority was peddling its votes for a vitally needed war program and exacting a heavy price.

For many members of the farm bloc the 110 per cent of parity provision was not enough. The struggle raged around three other formulae for giving special price status to growers of certain products. One of these would bar the administrator from setting maximum prices for farm commodities below the market price prevailing for such commodities on October 1, 1941. Another formula added the date of December 15, 1941, and the third added the average price for such commodities in the period July 1, 1919, to June 30, 1929, as still another alternative.

There was little attempt to conceal the crass basis on which these provisions were considered. Cotton farmers and sheep growers would do best under the 1919-1929 formula, so their representatives fought for that provision. Producers of wheat, corn, oats, barley, hogs, and butterfat were due to gain highest prices under the 110 per cent of parity clause. So would flue-cured tobacco, but burley tobacco would gain most from the October 1 or December 15 dispensations. Raisers of veal calves and beef cattle looked to the December 15 provision for their chief protection, as did the wool producers. Beef senators like O'Mahoney of Wyoming, cotton senators like Russell of Georgia, tobacco senators like Barkley of Kentucky, and other farm representatives, acted accordingly. By skillfully combining these clauses into one blanket provision, their backers were easily able to gain Senate approval.

Still the farm bloc was not content. Arousing even more controversy than the agricultural price schedules was an amendment introduced by Senator John H. Bankhead of Alabama providing that the price administrator could set no farm price ceiling without first receiving permission from the Secretary of Agriculture. Agricultural organizations have usually had a major influence in the Agriculture Department, and Claude R. Wickard, then Secretary, proved his loyalty to them by quietly supporting the Bankhead amendment even when the President was known to be decidedly opposed to it.

Open enemies of any form of price control, such as Senator W. Lee O'Daniel of Texas, warmly greeted the Bankhead provision.[10] Although majority leader Barkley read a letter from Mr. Roosevelt objecting to the amendment, the Senate accepted it, 48-37. So riddled with amendments that Barkley scornfully labeled it a "farm relief measure," the price control bill passed the Senate on January 10, 1942. Gerald P. Nye of North Dakota was the only senator to vote "Nay."

The President was keenly disappointed in the bill. He was incensed especially at an amendment that Senator O'Mahoney had inserted into the blanket farm provision; this amendment would have tied farm prices to wage levels and, according to O'Mahoney, would give farmers "about 120 per cent of parity."[11] Mr. Roosevelt intimated that he would veto the bill if it embodied this "wage-parity" formula. Shortly after the House and Senate conferees were appointed, he took the unusual step of calling the House members to his office in an attempt to induce them to modify the extreme farm provisions adopted by the Senate.

President Roosevelt showed his willingness to act on the wage front by establishing a National War Labor Board with power

10. *Congressional Record*, January 7, 1942, p. 110.
11. *Ibid.*, January 10, 1942, p. 220.

to stabilize wages. The Chief Executive was more troubled by the O'Mahoney than the Bankhead amendment; if he had any difficulty with the price administrator or the Secretary of Agriculture on the latter amendment, he could "fire either of them," he told reporters.

After a series of long and bitter sessions, the conference committee, with two Republicans dissenting, agreed on a bill that was stronger than either the original House or Senate measures. The gist of the O'Mahoney amendment was struck out, and the licensing and "buy-sell" provisions were retained. On the other hand, the four special formulae for pricing farm commodities remained in the bill, along with the veto power of the Secretary of Agriculture.

On January 26, 1942, the House passed this version, 289-114, after a motion to recommit had failed by a perilously narrow margin, 189-210. Thus many Representatives voted on both sides of the issue. A day later the Senate concurred, 65-14. Despite the urging of at least one high official in the Price Division that he veto the bill, the President signed it on January 29, 1942. Perhaps he knew even then that he would have to ask Congress to hold prices at parity—a move that he made in three months.

"In my judgment," Senator Bankhead said, "it is the best possible bill for the farmers that could be produced in the present legislative situation."[12]

MVA—ONE VALLEY OR TWO

IN SEPTEMBER 1944, at the height of a world war and during a presidential campaign, President Roosevelt urged on Congress "careful and early" consideration of a Missouri Valley Authority "for the greatest benefit of its citizens both present and future, and for the greatest benefit of the United States." Intimately touching the economic interests of diverse groups throughout the valley, this proposal intensified the political struggle inside

12. *Ibid.*, January 27, 1942, p. 725.

and outside the Missouri basin over the devices to be used to harness the river and develop the valley.

The Missouri river and its tributaries drain over half a million square miles of land, an area about one-sixth that of the United States. The river flows 2460 miles from its source in southwestern Montana to meet with the Mississippi 17 miles above St. Louis. The economy of the valley is highly varied. The land in the western and northern third of the valley is useful mainly for grazing and for mining; in the central portion the soil is more productive and the population greater, although there are alternate periods of drought and fertility; while a fairly stable industrial and agricultural economy is centered in the eastern and lower part of the valley.

Speaking broadly, the trouble with the valley is that its northern and western portions suffer from too little water, its lower part from too much. In the 1930's acute droughts afflicted the northwestern areas, while in the early 1940's floods cost the lower part of the valley $150,000,000 and many lives. These are the most important problems, but others exist: heavy erosion of soil; inadequate water supply for the larger cities; navigation difficulties on the lower river; stream pollution; and failure to develop fully the potentialities of power, recreation, and fish and wildlife.

The natural diversities in the Missouri valley have led to political disunity among its people. One common river flows through the whole area, but it is hardly a unifying element. People in the valley have tended to view the river in terms of their own particular local problems, rather than as a problem or challenge for the valley as a whole. The sharpest political cleavage is between inhabitants of the semi-arid areas of the upper valley and those of the more populated areas in the lower part. This hostility is decades old. The upper valley would exploit the Missouri for irrigation purposes, the lower valley wants the water for navigation. The former protests any widening or deepening of channels which, it fears, will deprive it of its vital water supply. The latter demands sufficient water for efficient navigation of the lower river.

There are other political differences and interest groups in the valley. Navigation work is linked closely to flood control, and it gains support from past and potential flood victims along the banks of the lower Missouri. Contractors throughout the valley have enormous vested interests in governmental development work and in the manner in which it is administered. Railroads face potential competition in the opening up of river transport. There are farmers eager for public power development; there are private utilities opposed to public power. Livestock raisers and mine operators are concerned with irrigation works. Each of these interests is represented by active and publicity-wise associations, enjoying understandings and alliances with other associations, and constantly struggling for the allegiance of the thousands of "neutrals." Each is represented in Congress.

The story of MVA is that of an attempt to meet the problems of the valley by a regional program for the sake of the people as a whole, and of how the effort was balked by a coalition of pressure politicians in the Senate, organized interest groups in the valley, and bureaucrats with vested interests in the existing piecemeal handling of the problems of the Missouri.

On May 15, 1944, the *St. Louis Post-Dispatch* printed an eloquent editorial addressed to newspaper editors throughout the Missouri Valley. Confessing its own error of having been preoccupied with the interests of its own section to the exclusion of other sections of the Missouri, the newspaper asked the editors to forsake parochial attitudes and to support a regional approach to a common problem: "With unity we can conquer the one big problem that the one big river challenges us to solve." This idea received scattered support in the valley. The National Farmers' Union, the CIO, and the AFL were enthusiastic over an MVA, but a number of important newspapers were hostile to the idea, and supporters of irrigation, navigation, and flood control were generally opposed or apathetic.

Senator James E. Murray of Montana introduced a bill for a Missouri Valley Authority in the Senate on August 18, 1944. The broad scope of the measure was indicated by its preamble: "To establish a Missouri Valley Authority to provide for unified water control and resource development on the Missouri River and surrounding region in the interest of the control and prevention of floods, the promotion of navigation and reclamation of the public lands, the promotion of family-type farming, the development of the recreational possibilities and the promotion of the general welfare of the area, the strengthening of the national defense, and for other purposes."

The proposed authority was directly modeled after the TVA. A board of three directors, enjoying considerable administrative autonomy, would administer the corporation at offices in the region. Although there were sharp differences between the Tennessee and Missouri valleys in topography, climate, and other respects, MVA supporters felt that the TVA idea was flexible enough to meet the particular problems of the Missouri valley too.

Murray's action came at a time when the irrigation and navigation interests were fighting each other with renewed intensity. Hostilities revolved around two plans for developing the valley. One of these had been advanced late in 1943 by the Corps of Engineers; it called for a series of dams and levees on the Missouri and was designed chiefly to meet navigation and flood control problems on the lower river. This was called the Pick plan, after its author, Colonel Lewis A. Pick, Army engineer at Omaha, Nebraska. The other plan, named the Sloan plan after an official in the Bureau of Reclamation, was concerned mainly with irrigation of several million acres of new land. The Missouri valley rang with charges and countercharges by irrigation and navigation interests that the other side was attempting to monopolize the water supply.

The specter of the MVA on the horizon had the immediate effect of uniting the contending forces. Proponents of the Pick and Sloan plans realized that only by a joint fight against the MVA could they stave off a plan that had received the powerful backing of the President. Truce parties from the Corps of Engineers and the Bureau of Reclamation met in Omaha late in October 1944 to patch up their differences. The resulting compromise was a rough division of territory and function that left the thorniest issues in the air. "A shotgun wedding," raged MVA proponents.

The *Post-Dispatch* said: "This is a marriage of convenience, arranged not only to kill off MVA but to save the interests jealously guarded by two powerful Government agencies." Nevertheless, the reconciliation plan was part of the flood control act that became law on December 22, 1944.

Meanwhile, Senator Murray was making little progress with his MVA bill. He had considered attaching it to the flood control bill, but he was dissuaded from this course when Senator John H. Overton of Louisiana, a representative of the navigation and flood control interests, promised speedy action on MVA in the new Congress. When Murray introduced a new MVA bill in the Senate in February 1945, however, he immediately met dilatory tactics.

The Montana senator had hoped that the new bill could be referred to the Committee on Agriculture and Forestry, but the Commerce Committee and the Irrigation and Reclamation Committee also claimed jurisdiction. Each of these committees had a major interest in the proposed legislation. As a result, the bill was referred to all three committees, each of which was to have 60 days to consider it. This action virtually doomed the chances of MVA during the 1945 session of Congress. The Commerce and Irrigation committees were known to be hostile to the measure, and they were to consider it first. President Roosevelt's death shortly before the first hearings on the bill made the bill's prospects seem even slimmer.

A subcommittee of the Commerce Committee was set up, under the chairmanship of Senator Overton, to consider MVA.

From the start Overton made no attempt to conceal his hostility to Murray's bill, nor did other members of the subcommittee. Following Murray's opening statement, there were three days of testimony by representatives of labor and liberal farm groups favoring the measure. Opposition to the bill was expressed by spokesmen for many diverse interests throughout the valley.

Representative William M. Whittington of Mississippi led off the attack as chairman of the Flood Control Committee of the House of Representatives, vice president of the National Rivers and Harbors Congress, and vice president of the Mississippi Valley Flood Control Association. He was seconded by many other representatives of special interests: the director of the National Rivers and Harbors Congress, who was also president of the Intercoastal Canal Association of Louisiana and Texas; the chairman of the River Development Committee for the Omaha area; the president of the American Waterways Operators, Inc.; the vice president of the National Reclamation Association; the president of the Nebraska Farm Bureau Federation, who was also president of the Producers Livestock Marketing Association of Omaha; and a score of others. Resolutions of opposition to MVA were submitted from automobile, lumbermen's, stock growers', dude ranchers', fish and game, and other associations.

The foes of MVA presented many arguments against it, but one common assumption ran through their testimony. This was their belief that MVA would not meet the special needs of their associations or areas. For example, Representative Whittington declared: "As representative of the lower Mississippi Valley, and as advocate of national flood control, I oppose the proposed Missouri Valley Authority and other similar authorities as they could be so operated as to prevent adequate flood control in the lower Mississippi Valley ..." A spokesman for the Montana Reclamation Association feared that MVA would emphasize production of power over the needs of irrigation. The managing director of the Associated General Contractors of America, Inc., based his organization's opposition to the bill primarily on the ground that MVA would undertake construction work with its own personnel, while the Engineers and the Reclamation Bureau let out much of their work to contractors.

This attitude reflected a concern with the interests of one's immediate group or area, an unwillingness to think in terms of the good of the valley as a whole. It stemmed from the fact that almost all the witnesses represented particular interests or localities in the valley. Senators spoke for their states, Representatives for their districts. But no one represented the whole valley. Senator Edwin C. Johnson of Colorado, arguing that "God Almighty divided that river into different parts," even went so far as to offer an amendment to MVA that would separate the river into the upper Missouri and the lower Missouri. Ordinarily one expects political machinery to be adapted to the problems that society faces. Here was a proposal, soberly put forward, to cut the problem down to the size of a particular committee system.

The special interests received vigorous support from Federal officials who operated agencies in the Missouri valley. Along with the Reclamation Bureau, the Interior Department had many units administering services there, such as the Fish and Wildlife Service, the Bureau of Mines, the Geological Survey, the General Land Office, the Grazing Service, the Office of Indian Affairs, and the National Park Service. Secretary of the Interior Harold L. Ickes testified against the MVA bill, and he was of course backed up by his agency heads. The Chief of Engineers, noting that the Corps has supervised construction work for 120 years, also objected to the measure.

The full Commerce Committee reported the MVA bill adversely on May 7, 1945. Over four months later a subcommittee of the Senate Committee on Irrigation and Reclamation held hearings on the measure. Senator Overton was also chairman of this subcommittee, and the hearings generally followed the pattern of the previous ones. Aside from Overton, the members of the subcommittee represented irrigation-minded states. When witnesses attempted to discuss other than irrigation phases of the MVA bill, they were told that such testimony was outside the jurisdiction of the committee.

Thus the central idea of MVA—the valley-wide approach—could not be presented. On October 13, 1945, the Senate Committee on Irrigation and Reclamation reported adversely on the bill. The measure was then referred to the Senate Committee on Agriculture and Forestry, but no action was taken by that committee. MVA was finished, at least in the 79th Congress.

It was not the defeat of MVA but the way in which it was defeated that arouses concern over the legislative process. Both congressmen and administrators approached the problems of the Missouri valley in terms of their particular interests, functions, or localities. There was a failure to come to grips with the central conception of a valley-wide approach.

Since they were elected from single states, the Senators acted only for organized groups in their states rather than for the valley as a whole and its unorganized inhabitants. Except for the President, no political institution seemed capable of acting for the whole valley; the committees failed miserably in this respect. There was not even a full-dress debate or a vote in the Senate, nor a real confrontation of the nation with the issue. MVA was quietly stifled in committee.

VI

꜖꜖꜖꜖꜖꜖꜖꜖꜖꜖꜖꜖꜖꜖꜖꜖꜖꜖꜖꜖꜖꜖꜖꜖꜖

Congressmen As Overseers

THE story of three bills in the previous chapter underlines some of the main Congressional failings. These failings can be summed up in a few words—the frequent incapacity to act decisively in the face of pressures from organized minorities. The job of Congress, however, is not simply a legislative one. It also supervises the administration of tens of thousands of statutes by the vast and far-flung bureaucracy of the administrative state. Many members of Congress spend more time overseeing the departments and bureaus than writing or debating laws.

It is not surprising that the legislators take their supervisory role seriously, for they have an immense political stake in the operations of the bureaucracy. Governmental activities affect the fortunes of voters in every state and district in the nation. If there is friction between the administrative state and the Congressman's constituents, he is usually the first to hear of it. Often he must serve as intermediary or buffer. Naturally he works to maintain some hold on the officials who tax, subsidize, regulate, restrict, promote, and service the folks back home.

There is another and more important reason for Congressional concern with administration. Government officials have large discretionary powers; it has long been a commonplace that the manner in which law is applied is often as important as the law itself. The managers of "big government" have it within their power to help shape the economic, social, and physical contours of America during the years ahead. This is a power that Congress regards jealously, and well it might, for the legislators hold themselves ultimately responsible to the voters for the manner in which the laws are carried out.

WHO'S IN CHARGE HERE?

BUT the President, too, is responsible to the voters, and the Constitution vested the executive power in him. The Founding Fathers did not, however, clearly distinguish between the President's executive authority and the supervisory powers of Congress over administration. On the contrary, they deliberately divided administrative power between the two branches as part of the system of checks and balances. Thus the stage was set from the beginning for tussles between President and Congress over control of the administrative apparatus. Responding to different patterns of political forces, the Chief Executive and the legislators inevitably have tried to employ that apparatus for different purposes.

This division of authority has serious implications for American democracy. The big job facing democrats is to keep our huge bureaucracy responsible to the majority. It is bootless at this stage to deplore the existence of the administrative state. It exists; and all signs point to its continued existence and aggrandizement. The vital question concerns the objectives that its army of officials will pursue.

Thus a bureaucracy can be employed for the benefit of a military caste or of an economic or social elite. It can be a tool for realizing the democratic aspirations of a community, or a means of consolidating a despotism. It may serve majority or minority purposes, or a mixture of both.

This is not to say that a bureaucracy is a neutral mechanism. It will not serve democracy one day, and dictatorship the next. All sorts of internal checks and forces give it some momentum

and direction of its own. But in the long run, the administrative
state will serve those who possess political and economic power,
although a host of administrative managers, directors, and technicians will seem to hold the reins of state.[1]

The issue in the United States is whether the bureaucracy will
be responsible mainly to the majority of the voters through the
President, or mainly to organized minorities through key individuals and committees in Congress. Majority rule has suffered as a
result of the division of administrative control between President
and Congress. Neither Senate nor House is so constituted as to
reflect majority sentiment fairly, as described above. Moreover,
in practice the full houses of Congress cannot supervise the administrative agencies; the job must necessarily be delegated to
committees and individual members, who are often even less
equipped to speak for a majority of the voters than the whole
Congress.

"If the representative body attempts to assume the executive
function," Professor Key has written, "it tends to become a market place where individuals and factions bargain away the national welfare for sectional or parochial gain."[2] In the United
States, the legislative body has not only attempted to assume the
executive function. It has succeeded in doing so to a large extent.
What are the controls that it exercises over the bureaucracy?

In the first place, as the law-making body Congress enacts,
repeals, and amends the laws under which the administrative
agencies operate. Usually Congress delegates a great deal of administrative discretion to the President, who re-delegates it to
his subordinates. But Congress delegates only to the extent it
wishes to do so. If they prefer, the legislators can write a set of
detailed legislative standards that will bind the agency at every

1. Cf. James Burnham, *The Managerial Revolution* (New York: The
John Day Co., 1941).

2. V. O. Key, "Legislative Control," in Morstein Marx (ed.), *Elements of
Public Administration* (New York: Prentice-Hall, Inc., 1946), p. 339.

turn. They can specify how the agency shall be organized and controlled, how it shall be operated. The establishment of a powerful general counsel in the National Labor Relations Board under the Taft-Hartley Act, for example, was designed to affect vitally the manner in which the labor law was administered, as it has done in fact.

The Supreme Court has staked out general limits beyond which power cannot be delegated; as Justice Cardozo said years ago, the President has no "roving commission" to do anything he pleases.[3] But there is no constitutional limit on the power of Congress to refuse to delegate administrative authority. Failure to delegate may be as serious a matter in the long run as excessive delegation.

Legislative control over administration is enhanced by the power of Congress to revoke grants of authority or to set time limits. Congress has specified in some acts that they would remain in effect until Congress ended them by concurrent resolution. Since concurrent resolutions do not require the President's signature, this was a means of insuring legislative control over the duration of administrative authority.[4] The best known example of short-term legislation established under time limits is the Reciprocal Trade program. Under such an arrangement Congress exercises power through the easiest and most convenient means at its disposal—the failure to take positive action.

Secondly, Congress shares in the executive function through its investigations. Congressional probes range in nature from full-dress and ritualistic examinations of officials in extended hearings before press and public, to interrogations of a few officials in the privacy of a congressman's office. They may be based on months of combing of the agency's files by a large congressional staff, or

3. Dissenting opinion of Mr. Justice Cardozo, *Panama Refining Co. v. Ryan,* 293 U.S. 388, 435 (1935).
4. See Howard White, "Executive Responsibility to Congress via Concurrent Resolution," *American Political Science Review,* 1942, Vol. 36, pp. 895-900. The constitutionality of this device has not yet been tested.

they may stem from a random "fishing expedition" by one or two congressmen who happen to be interested in the agency's operations. They may be designed to unearth all the relevant facts as a basis for further legislation, or they may be intended to vilify a particular agency, its officials, and its program.

In any event, congressional investigations are effective—if cumbersome and expensive—means of control. Administrators dread investigations: the time lost, the disruption of administrative routine, the certainty that some lapses will come to light, the likelihood that the agency will end up being suspect even if it is exonerated of the major charges brought against it. Many of them prefer to make changes in their policies or even in personnel to head off such an enterprise. Thus the mere threat of investigation becomes a form of executive control by congressmen.

A third means of legislative control of administration is congressional influence over personnel. The President has a fairly free hand in choosing members of his Cabinet, but his selection of the hosts of commissioners, bureau chiefs, and other administrators at the secondary level is strongly affected by the views of powerful factions or individuals in House and Senate. The upper chamber, of course, must confirm presidential appointments to a number of offices, but legislative influence goes further than this.

Through the device of "senatorial courtesy" both Senators and Representatives share in the appointment of important Federal officials in their states and districts. Congress can force the resignation of administrators by setting up a drumfire of criticism on Capitol Hill. Ultimately, there is the power of impeachment, or at least the threat of impeachment.

On balance, Congress has more power over the appointment of personnel than their removal. Investigations, concentrated criticism, and the power of impeachment are inefficient weapons that are all too likely to backfire. As Professor Key has said, "There is no clean-cut method by which the legislature can simply say, 'We have nothing against you personally. Nor do we question your competence or your Americanism. Our views on what the policy of your department should be are not the same as yours. You are fired.' "[5]

THE PURSE AND ITS STRINGS

THESE three methods of Congressional supervision of administration—direct policy-making, investigating, "hiring and firing" —are significant but not always reliable means of influencing executive actions. They tend to be sporadic and negative in their impact, and sometimes self-defeating. Shrewd administrators can often get around even the most precise statutory language if they feel it unduly hampers their programs. Investigations take place after the fact and have an uncertain effect on future administration; forced retirement of an official does not insure that his successor will be any better from the legislator's viewpoint.

Given the congressmen's stake in administration, it is not surprising that they have exploited increasingly another instrument of control—one that is more positive and systematic and sure. This is the control of appropriations. The appropriating process has come to be one of the chief ways whereby Congress, in Macmahon's words, is asserting the "right of continuous intervention" in administrative affairs.[6] For the congressional purse has strings that tie the administrators to those legislators who control it.

The appropriating process greatly fortifies each of the three techniques of control described above: It is a means of formally expressing congressional policy; it provides a sharp edge for the investigatory weapon; it can be used to influence the appointment and discharge of personnel. Each of these uses of the appropriating power merits further attention.

The job of congressional policy-making is split between two sets of committees, legislative (or authorizing) and appropriat-

5. *Op. cit.*, Morstein Marx, ed., p. 357.
6. A. W. Macmahon, "Congressional Oversight of Administration: The Power of the Purse," *Political Science Quarterly*, Vol. LVIII, No. 2, June 1943, p. 163.

ing. The legislative committees are supposed to set forth policy, and the appropriations committees to authorize the necessary funds, but no such simple division of power exists. For the appropriations committees can deny funds to carry out projects that a legislative committee and a majority of Congress have endorsed. The appropriators have a veto over the authorizers. They have a veto, moreover, which they can exercise at least once a year.

This split authority was dramatized in the handling of the European Recovery Program. During late 1947 and early 1948 an epic debate had taken place in the halls of Congress and throughout the nation over this crucial issue of foreign policy. After polls showed a strong majority of the voters in favor of the plan, Congress passed the bill overwhelmingly in each House, authorizing several billions for the first year. But then it was discovered—to the chagrin of those who did not know of the final appropriations hurdle—that the fight for ERP was by no means over. The needed funds still had to be secured by a separate act of Congress, and it developed that Chairman John Taber of the House Appropriations committee continued to view ERP with misgivings. Anxious weeks went by before the committee, under heavy pressure from both parties, granted the funds, but as a toll it exacted a reduction of several hundred millions.

The more typical method of policy-making by appropriations committeemen is not through outright vetoes, but through detailing how funds shall be apportioned to various activities. This is the most positive and flexible single method of legislative control of administration.

The appropriators can be niggardly with agencies or units whose policies or programs they dislike; they can subsidize heavily the functions that they favor. They do not, of course, have a free hand in this respect, for potent groups of voters that benefit from certain governmental services will come to the aid of the bureaucrats who serve them. This has often been the experience of agencies ministering to such articulate groups as farmers and veterans. But in general, so wide is the net cast by the appropriations committeemen, so strategic their position, so quiet and un-spectacular their operations, and so technical their work, that their shadows lie athwart the whole administrative structure.

Nor does their power derive merely from the allotment of funds. An appropriations act is not simply a listing of sums; it usually embodies a series of legislative directions. These may be trivial in nature; thus a recent agricultural appropriations act provided that, with certain exceptions, "no part of the funds appropriated by this Act shall be expended in the purchase of twine manufactured from commodities or materials purchased outside of the United States."[7]

If congressmen in influential positions are opposed to crop forecasting by the Department of Agriculture, they can rule—as they have done—that no funds shall be used to pay any official for that purpose.[8] Often these legislative directions are of greater significance, as in recent cases where officials have been instructed to adopt certain administrative policies or practices.[9]

An extreme version of this kind of direction is the legislative rider, which often embodies administrative controls. The riders may or may not have anything to do with the appropriations bill they are tacked onto. Since they cannot be vetoed without sacrificing the whole bill, a President usually has no recourse but to sign the bill, including the rider, with a protest.

The appropriations committeemen are not content to state their views once a year and then to leave the administrators to their own devices. Knowing the importance of sustained direction, many of the legislators bolster their formal powers with informal meetings with administrative chiefs around the year. These meetings may take place at lunch, in the congressman's or administrator's office, or more formally in the committee room. The appropriators often take a paternalistic attitude toward agencies under their wing. They feel free to offer directions and

7. Public Law 712, 80th Congress, 2nd Sess., 1948.
8. *Ibid.*
9. See, for example, House Report No. 2200, pp. 8-9, 77th Cong., 2nd Sess.

suggestions, and usually they expect their conception of administration to be followed out. Sometimes they require periodic reports from the agencies to insure that their directions are put into effect.

The relations of administrator and appropriator are not necessarily antagonistic; occasionally the former may go on his own initiative to Capitol Hill, as a protective tactic to gain support for a proposed action. While the nature and extent of 'round-the-year supervision by appropriations committees varies from committee to committee and from agency to agency and from year to year, this type of legislative oversight has increased measurably in recent years.[10]

The appropriations committeemen are authorized to probe deeply into the agencies' affairs—so deeply that their investigations often rival those of legislative committees in significance and duration. In hearings lasting days and sometimes weeks, departmental officers are cross-examined intensively on their past expenditures and future needs. Yet the investigations often lack precision and planning. As Galloway points out, "the questions tend to be of a random, impromptu character, picking on this or that item in a spot-check quest for information."[11] Often the chief result is frustration on both sides.

Finally, the appropriators sometimes try to control selection of personnel. This may be done affirmatively through informal suggestions on patronage matters; it has even been tried negatively in formal acts. A relief appropriations act passed in 1941 specified that none of the funds might be used to pay a named individual, who happened to be the former head of the Workers' Alliance.[12] The same result can be reached, of course, by abolishing the unit in which an official works, but such "ripper legislation" is an awkward method if Congress wishes to continue the service involved.

10. Macmahon found in 1943 that, generally speaking, interim supervisory relationships were increasing. *Op. cit.,* p. 407.

11. *Op. cit.,* p. 247.

12. Cited by Macmahon, *op. cit.,* p. 167.

A more notable effort to discharge personnel occurred in 1943, when a section of a deficiency appropriations act provided that none of the funds could be used to pay three employees of the Federal Communications Commission, Goodwin B. Watson, William E. Dodd, Jr., and Robert Morss Lovett.[13]

The voiding of this section by the Supreme Court has forced the appropriations committeemen to fall back on slightly less obvious methods of controlling personnel. An appropriations measure in 1948 stipulated that the Commissioner of Reclamation and his regional directors must have at least five years of professional engineering experience.[14] This provision was directed at the Commissioner and a regional director who were not engineers and with whose administration of the law the appropriations committeemen happened to differ.

How Congress can use a combination of methods to control the agencies was illustrated a few years ago in the case of "Cox vs. FCC." This case was not typical of congressional behavior, fortunately, but it does indicate the variety of weapons that Congress can employ in a pitched battle.

In 1942 the Federal Communications Commission discovered that Representative Eugene Cox of Georgia had been paid $2,500 for legal services in Washington by a radio station applying for renewal of its license. Under a federal statute, acceptance of this fee was a criminal offense. After the FCC referred the matter to the Department of Justice, the following events occurred:

(1) Mr. Cox introduced a resolution to investigate the FCC.

(2) The resolution was quickly passed by the House and Mr. Cox himself was named chairman of the investigating committee.

(3) The investigation, bearing all the marks of a simple "fishing expedition," continued for months. Ultimately Cox was forced to resign.

13. F. L. Schuman, " 'Bill of Attainder' in the Seventy-Eighth Congress," *American Political Science Review*, 1943, Vol. 37, pp. 819-829.
14. Public Law 841, 80th Cong., 2nd Sess., p. 16.

(4) The Watson-Dodd-Lovett "bill of attainder" was then passed over the President's objections.

(5) The House Appropriations Committee recommended a straight 25 per cent cut in the FCC's whole appropriation, and the House approved.

(6) The Senate Appropriations Committee, headed by Senator McKellar, recommended a further reduction of $500,000. The Senate approved. The deep cuts were retained in conference committee virtually intact.[15]

In the light of an incident like this, it is hardly surprising that administrators think twice before defying a powerfully placed congressman or committee, no matter how great the provocation.

THE PRICE OF SEMI-INDEPENDENCE

THE independent regulatory agencies present the problem of congressional control of administration in one of its most acute forms. For many years students of government have been troubled by the anomalous status of the Interstate Commerce Commission, the Federal Trade Commission, the Federal Reserve Board, and a half dozen other independent establishments. The problem is not simply one of administrative organization. It is far more serious, for it falls squarely into the area of Presidential-Congressional relationships.

It has been said that our independent agencies, like the British Empire, grew up in a fit of absent-mindedness. It can also be said of these agencies, as the whole Executive Branch was once described in a famous phrase, that they have "grown up without plan or design like the barns, shacks, silos, tool sheds, and garages of an old farm."[16] Looking back on the rise of the independent regulatory establishments over the past sixty years, one

15. R. D. Leigh, "Politicians vs. Bureaucrats," *Harper's Magazine,* Vol. 190, No. 1136, Jan. 1945, pp. 97-105. Mr. Leigh served with the FCC in 1942-1944.

16. President's Committee on Administrative Management, *Report,* Washington, D. C., 1937, p. 32.

finds both these statements suggestive. One can discern also, however, a certain purposefulness in that growth.

In setting up the "headless fourth branch" of government Congress at times has seemed unaware of the implications of its acts for the traditional separation of powers among three organs of government. The ICC—the first such agency—was established in 1887 without a real confrontation by Congress of the basic issues involved, such as the new agency's relation to the three branches of government, and its commingling of executive, legislative, and judicial powers.[17] In subsequent years Congress has assigned some regulatory functions to the Executive departments, such as the Department of Agriculture, and other such functions to the independent commissions, in a seemingly haphazard and inconsistent manner. Nevertheless, one basic motive is evident almost all the way through the sixty years—the desire of the legislative branch to make these independent agencies largely immune to direct presidential and partisan control.

This separation from the President has been accomplished mainly through limiting the Chief Executive's power to "hire and fire." His appointments of commissioners and board members are subject to Senate confirmation. Furthermore, Congress has often fenced in his power of choice by writing into the statutes qualifications relating to party membership, residence, or professional experience. More important, the members have staggered terms so that a President may find, on taking office, that a commission is dominated by administrative lame ducks, and that he must wait a year or two before he may expect a majority more friendly to his policies.

The President has some power to remove members "for cause," but the extent of that power is not clear,[18] and the Supreme Court's invalidation of Franklin D. Roosevelt's ousting of Commissioner Humphrey from the Federal Trade Commission in-

17. R. E. Cushman, *The Independent Regulatory Commissions* (New York: Oxford University Press, 1941), pp. 58-62. This section draws heavily on Professor Cushman's exhaustive analysis.

18. Cushman, *op. cit.,* pp. 463 ff.

dicates that the President cannot remove commissioners because they are not in harmony with his policies. The legal gap between President and commission is deepened by a physical one: generally the independent establishments have been outside the line departments, even on "housekeeping" matters. All this is bolstered by a tradition and psychology of independence.

Over the long run, at least, this independence of the President is not absolute. Unless the Senate balks at his appointments, he ultimately will exercise some control over the agencies through choosing members who reflect his own political views. The problem, however, concerns the short run—the first one or two years of a new Administration when a Chief Executive may wish to give purposefulness and direction to the whole bureaucracy, including the independent establishments. Every President may not be so fortunate or skillful as Franklin D. Roosevelt, who abolished one commission, reduced the powers of another, secured the resignation of the chairman of a third, and, despite Mr. Humphrey, had by June 1934 appointed all five members of the Federal Trade Commission.[19]

The difficulty has been compounded by the mushrooming of the independent regulatory establishments during the past fifteen years. New agencies include the Federal Power Commission, the Securities and Exchange Commission, the Federal Communications Commission, the National Labor Relations Board, the Maritime Commission, and the Civil Aeronautics Authority. "There are no more important tasks being done by the federal government than those which have been assigned to the independent regulatory commissions," Cushman says. "None affect more vitally the economic life of the nation."[20] A newly elected President, trying to cope with depression or inflation, might find some of the most important economic controls in the hands of

19. E. P. Herring, *Public Administration and the Public Interest* (New York: McGraw-Hill Book Co., 1936), pp. 222-223.
20. Cushman, *op. cit.*, p. 5.

officials hostile or indifferent to his program, especially in a time of political tension and factionalism.

The problem is also one of every-day coordination of policy and administration. At a thousand points the programs and operations of the independent agencies bear upon those of the rest of the Executive branch. Consider the Maritime Commission, for example. In time of war it has a vital role in the designing and building of ships. In peacetime its operations bring it into frequent contact with the State Department, through its awarding of subsidies, its selling of ships abroad, its investigation of foreign shipping and port practices, its regulation of routes and services, and its participation in international enterprises. Further functions of the Commission involve labor relations, procurement, contracting, financing, training, research, designing, insuring, renegotiating, and many others that relate closely to similar problems encountered by other agencies.[21]

What has been the result of this semi-independence? The result has not been—despite hopes to the contrary—to take these regulatory agencies "out of politics." Agencies with such tremendous powers cannot exist in a political vacuum. On the contrary, in their legislative and administrative activities they have been subjected to a maze of pressures—pressures from the industry regulated, from the groups on whose behalf the industry is regulated, from the interested public, from the political parties, from officials in the executive and legislative branches, from other independent agencies.

The main result of semi-independence has simply been to alter the type of pressure that can be brought to bear effectively on the agencies. It has been to make them less responsive to majority rule and more susceptible to minority rule. More precisely, the result has been to make the agencies less responsible to the official playing majority politics—i.e., the President—and more

21. For further comment on the question of coordination, see J. W. Fesler, in Morstein Marx (ed.), *op. cit.,* pp. 228-229.

susceptible to those playing minority politics—i.e., members of Congress and industry representatives.

Necessarily the price of semi-independence is high. Harmony of every-day operations suffers. Harmony of over-all policy suffers. Governmental planning in important fields is impeded.[22] More important, the independent regulatory establishments are sheltered from fresh currents of public opinion, and from majority sentiment as reflected in presidential leadership. As a result, they give in to inertia, or they become exposed to the influence of the regulated interests.[23]

It has been argued that since the independent regulatory agencies are "arms" of Congress, coordination and unity of purpose can be achieved by the legislative branch. Unfortunately, Congress is not able to do the job. Policy-making in the fields of the independent agencies is divided between House and Senate and among a multitude of committees and chairmen in each chamber. Supervision of the agencies is further divided among the appropriations committees and subcommittees. These separate entities, which like to go their own way, would have to coordinate themselves before they could hope to integrate the policies and operations of the independent agencies with those of the rest of the government.

Despite their limitations in this respect, members of Congress take a proprietary attitude toward the commissions. In the absence of presidential control of the commissions, the legislators have found it easier to move in on the exposed agencies. The means of control discussed above—statute-making, investigations, selection and removal of personnel, the power of the purse —have been employed to the full.

Repeatedly Presidents have attempted to direct the commissions; their frequent failures are tributes to the strength of congressional backing. Congress stands behind the "headless fourth branch"; it "has not hesitated to give to the independent com-

22. Cushman, *op. cit.,* pp. 727-741.
23. Fesler, *op. cit.,* p. 230.

missions any jobs which could be conveniently dumped upon them."[24] It is not surprising that in two reorganization acts Congress has refused to give the President power to interfere with these agencies. Essentially, they are the creatures of Congress, which means that they are vulnerable to the organized groups that work through Congress.

THE ATOMIZATION OF AUTHORITY

WE RETURN to the central fact: the rivalry between President and Congress for mastery of the huge bureaucracy of our administrative state. It seems likely that as long as the two branches of government continue to respond to different political forces, the attempt to serve both these masters will induce internal stresses in the administrative machinery.

Admittedly, the issue of divided responsibility does not lie simply between President and Congress. Even if there were no House or Senate, the President would be hard put to control the hundreds of agencies and the thousands of administrators under his nominal command. All kinds of centrifugal forces operate in an apparatus that serves—and is conditioned by—a free society. The President's marching orders encounter inertia, failure of communication, traditionalism, divided loyalties, the criss-crossing of authority stemming from informal organization, group solidarity and parochialism, excessive allegiance to clients and supporters.[25] Administrators are not automatons; they have a will and an ideology of their own.

24. Cushman, *op. cit.*, p. 459.
25. E. P. Herring, *Public Administration and the Public Interest,* Parts I and V. See also J. P. Comer, *Legislative Functions of National Administrative Authorities* (New York: Columbia University Press, 1927), pp. 199-200; Morstein Marx (ed.), *op. cit.*, chpts. 4, 8, 9, 13, 14, 22; and F. J. Roethlisberger and W. J. Dickson, *Management and the Worker* (Cambridge: Harvard University Press, 1939); Ordway Tead, *Democratic Administration* (New York: Association Press, 1945); C. I. Barnard, *The Functions of the Executive* (Cambridge: Harvard University Press, 1938); H. A. Simon, *Administrative Behavior* (New York: The MacMillan Company, 1947).

Nevertheless, a Chief Executive with the aid of a capable staff can usually cope with these divisive factors. What he cannot do is to hold them in check when they are generated and sustained by blocs, committees, and individuals in the legislature. For we have reached a point where the President's formal means of controlling the administrators—i.e., direct policy-making, budgeting, personnel, reporting, supervising—are largely counterbalanced in each case by equivalent methods, as described above, at the disposal of the legislators.

The picture of the administrator who can elude Presidential control because he enjoys the backing of a powerful faction in Congress is one all too familiar to observers of the Washington scene.[26] The President who wishes to be Chief Executive in the real sense of the term must fall back on informal and extra-legal instruments of control, such as his political leadership and administrative dexterity, and these are not always dependable.[27]

The problem might be more manageable if it involved building a bridge merely between the President and the whole of the legislative branch. In practice, however, control of administration by Congress means control by two houses, and by numerous factions, committees, subcommittees, and individual members within those houses. For instance, an appropriations bill is formally acted upon by a subcommittee, by the full committee, and by the whole chamber. Actually, as Macmahon points out, the decisions that emerge are usually the work of a very few members of the subcommittee, assisted by veteran clerks.[28] Congressional majorities have little alternative but to ratify these decisions.

The result is an extreme fragmentation of power within Congress. And because lines of authority often run horizontally from congressman or committee to department or bureau chief, this dispersion of authority is reflected in the Executive branch, al-

26. V. O. Key in Marx (ed.), *op. cit.*, chpt. 15.
27. Cf. C. J. Friedrich, *Constitutional Government and Democracy* (Boston: Ginn and Company, 1946), pp. 401-413.
28. Macmahon, *op. cit.*, pp. 176-178, 386.

though to a lesser degree. Responsibility for policy and administration becomes shrouded in a fantastically complicated network
of ever shifting relationships among President, administrators,
staff agencies, Senate, House of Representatives, committees, subcommittees, chairmen, individual legislators, and among infinite
combinations and permutations thereof. "There is no danger in
power," Woodrow Wilson once wrote, "if only it be not irresponsible. If it be divided, dealt out in shares to many, it is obscured;
and if it be obscured, it is made irresponsible."[29]

This dispersion of authority is serious enough; equally grave is
the resulting influence over the administrative process vested in
congressmen who do not accept the assumptions of the administrative state. These assumptions are that our elaborate administrative apparatus is here to stay; that it must be at the service of
the great mass of the voters; that it must be given direction and
purposefulness; that it is a rather delicate mechanism and cannot
stand too much tampering. The legislator, with his immediate
political concerns, his enforced catering to minorities, his specialized interpretation of the general welfare,[30] his hostility toward non-elected experts holding power, is uneasy at the sight of
this looming bureaucracy.

He cannot abolish the administrative giant, because his own
colleagues will spring to the defense of the agencies that serve
their constituents. He can, however, undermine it. He can deny
sustenance to those functions around which no organized minority or congressional bloc will rally, but which in the long run will
determine the viability of democratic administration—namely,
planning, research, statistical and economic analysis, scientific investigation, administrative management, information, staffing.
He can, through investigations, parsimony, and his immunity
from libel suits, foster an administrative climate that will drive
the ablest officials out of government. Or if he cannot weaken the

29. *Political Science Quarterly,* Vol. 2, No. 1, June, 1887, p. 213.
30. L. D. White, "Legislative Responsibility for the Public Service," in
New Horizons in Public Administration (Alabama: University of Alabama
Press, 1945), pp. 7-10.

administrative structure, he can seek to turn it to his own purposes. The measure of his success in this final endeavor will be the extent to which the bureaucracy degenerates into a jumble of clashing principalities separately responsible to every group except a majority of the voters.

APPROACHES TO REFORM

THE traditional remedy for this guerrilla warfare between President and Congress over control of administration is for each to know its place—and to keep it. Under this formula, Congress should confine itself to over-all policy-making and planning, while the Executive branch should restrict itself to carrying out the plans and policies. Congress should not interfere with administrative details; administrators should keep out of politics. Congress, in short, should determine the ends; the bureaucracy should fashion the means.

The trouble with this formula is two-fold. In the first place, it rests on a distinction between law-making and law-executing, between politics and administration, that is increasingly recognized as a false one. In Gulick's phrase, the governing process is a "seamless web of discretion and action."[31] The great administrators usually must be great politicians as well. They must make important policy decisions with or without congressional sanction. For their part, congressmen find it politically inexpedient to keep their hands off administrative activities.

In the second place, this formula runs counter to the facts of the American system. It is all very well to argue that policy should be controlled by the "elected representatives of the

31. Luther Gulick, "Politics, Administration, and the New Deal," *Annals,* Sept. 1933, p. 61. See also C. J. Friedrich, "Public Policy and the Nature of Administrative Responsibility," *Public Policy* (Cambridge: Harvard University Press, 1940), Vol. I, p. 6; J. M. Gaus and L. O. Wolcott, *Public Administration and the United States Department of Agriculture* (Chicago: Public Administration Service, 1940); M. E. Dimock, *Modern Politics and Administration* (New York: 1937); and Dwight Waldo, *The Administrative State* (New York: The Ronald Press, 1948), esp. chpt. 7.

people" when all the representatives of the people are in the legislature. But in the United States the President is also the representative of the people, and a very powerful one too. He cannot possibly refrain from making crucial political decisions, nor can his subordinates. On the other hand, Congress will participate in administration as long as it seems politically desirable to do so. It has shown no disposition to leave the administrators to their own devices.

In short, power over policy-making and policy-executing has been irretrievably joined in both President and Congress, as a result of the unity and indivisibility of the governing process and the nature of our political system. The vital question is not whether we can assign different functions to each and insulate those functions in separate compartments. We cannot. The vital question is whether we can gain unity on broad objectives among the chief policy-makers in each branch of government.

The answer to this question in turn depends on whether or not Congress and the President respond to generally similar patterns of political forces. In Great Britain there is normally no sharp contest between the Cabinet and the majority in Commons for control of the civil service because both the members of Commons and the members of the Cabinet are answerable to the same broad grouping of the electorate as organized in the party in power. In the United States the President and Congress will work in unison when they, too, act in response to roughly the same majority of the voters.

Given such a basis of harmony between the legislative and executive branches,[32] a number of changes would improve the present state of affairs:

(1) Joint executive-legislative committees or councils could be established to examine and discuss broad questions of administrative policy-making, organization, and operations.

(2) Congressional committees supervising administration should be staffed by experts in the various fields. The job of the

32. See Chapter 11.

staff should not be to pry into all details of administration but to examine and report on the more important decisions and activities of the Executive branch. Their most important task would be to help coordinate the supervisory activities of members of Congress and of their committees.

(3) The British system of provisional orders might be adapted to American use. Under that system, certain types of administrative rulings lie before Parliament before becoming effective, and Parliament has various forms of veto power. Obviously, only the most important rules should be the concern of Congress.

(4) Procedures for reporting administrative action to Congress and to the people could be improved. At present masses of information go to Capitol Hill, but in a form that often conceals vital facts instead of emphasizing them. Improved reporting is the joint duty of administrator and legislative staff.

(5) Whether or not a harmony of outlook is achieved between President and Congress, the Chief Executive should possess the power to veto specific items in appropriation bills.[33] Most of the state governors have exercised this right, and there has been little abuse of it. The item veto should extend to legislative riders on appropriation bills, unless Congress itself adopts stringent rules against their use.

(6) Many of the operating and administrative functions of the independent boards and commissions should be transferred to Executive departments. For this purpose new agencies may have to be created, such as a Transportation Department. In particular the President should control those policies and actions of the independent establishments that relate to our foreign policies or that closely affect the economic stability of the nation.

33. Cf. Young, *op. cit.*, p. 235.

VII

Congress and the Coming Crisis

TO MEASURE Congress alongside the problems of yesterday or today is not enough. Like engineers who think in terms of the greatest possible stress on a dam or bridge, we must judge Congress in terms of its capacity to cope with a crisis situation.

What will be the nature of this crisis? At worst, we face sooner or later a long and bitter war, or series of wars. At best we will have peace, and the demobilization of war economies. Most likely we confront an extended period of "cold war," with all the economic stresses and strains that must come with it.

In any event—whether war, peace, or cold war—our economy faces a grave test. It may be, of course, that we have reached permanent prosperity. Undoubtedly our economic wisdom is far ahead of that of 1929. But there has been no basic alteration in our economy to shield it against the cycles of "boom and bust" that have plagued it for well over a century. A hard look at the future must note the likelihood of another economic crash. And since the United States is now the economic kingpin of the world, such an emergency would be world-wide in scope.

Economic crisis in America will mean political crisis as well. Considering the current threats to civil liberties in the United States and the domination of the media of communication by a few groups, there is some doubt that the people will be allowed

119

free discussion and exposure to competing ideas that form so vital a prelude to democratic action. But there is even more doubt as to the capacity of American government to act in response to deep popular needs. For action requires harmony between President and Congress.

Will the coming crisis, in political terms, be met by a united people standing shoulder to shoulder, or will it lead to an explosive condition of dissension among groups, resulting in paralysis? In governmental terms, will that crisis bring teamwork—or deadlock?

CONGRESS UNDER STRESS

IF HISTORY is any guide, Congress will be a center of stalemate and inaction in the event of another prolonged depression.

The great depression that began in 1929 was a test of the capacity of Congress to take the initiative with a broad program of relief and recovery. Occupying the White House was a President who believed that the independence of the legislature was the "militant safeguard to liberty." He would not intervene, except for pointing out areas where action was needed. But as the long years dragged by, Congress made only fitful efforts to cope with the crisis, and these proved hopelessly unequal to the demands of a deepening depression.

Too late Mr. Hoover forsook his mute role; in the latter part of his term his political plight was such that presidential leadership was impossible. And even in the last months of his administration, with the nation gripped by a paralyzing financial panic, Congress shunned its chance at leadership. Analyzing the final congressional session before Roosevelt took office, Professor Herring noted: "The necessities of the time called for cooperative planning and swift, united action, but the exigencies of politics suggested procrastination and obstruction. And the latter considerations prevailed."[1]

1. E. P. Herring, "Second Session of the Seventy-Second Congress," *The American Political Science Review,* Vol. XXVII, No. 3, June 1933, p. 404.

The inertness in Congress during the latter Hoover years stemmed partly from the fact that the Senate was under Republican control and the House under Democratic, although in both chambers the parties were almost even in strength. This situation made action difficult.

Yet Congress showed no more disposition to take leadership over policy during the Roosevelt years. With the Democrats holding huge majorities in both House and Senate, the legislators nevertheless accepted the President's direction after he proclaimed that he was ready to upset, if necessary, the "normal balance of executive and legislative authority" and to apply to Congress "discipline and direction" under his leadership. The Chief Executive became Chief Legislator as well.

This is not to say that Congress was always content to eat humble pie. The talk about a "rubber-stamp Congress," even in reference to the famous "Hundred Days," was often exaggerated. But during virtually the whole course of the Roosevelt administrations the Democrats in Congress allowed the President to block out the main lines of legislative action, to set the timing for consideration of new policy, and, for the most part, to fix even the details of the New Deal measures.

Although the legislators often amended the proposals sent over by the White House, and sometimes ratified them belatedly or refused to ratify them, the alternatives were never between a comprehensive presidential program and a comprehensive congressional program. The alternatives were a Roosevelt program or none at all.

Will history repeat itself with the coming of another depression? In the opinion of at least one member of Congress, it will. While discussing the reorganization of Congress with his colleagues on the La Follette-Monroney committee, Senator Pepper of Florida postulated a future situation of mounting unemployment calling for action via fiscal policy, public works, tariffs, "and a whole lot of things, nearly the whole circumference of the Government." Pepper went on:

What happens, except that we get some sporadic suggestions, somebody makes a speech, and somebody puts in a bill, somebody has an idea here and there, but what generally happens is we wait until the President formulates, through the executive agencies, what he thinks is the best approach to this thing.

Then we all wait around, not knowing what to do, and finally the President comes out, there are big headlines in the papers, and the President says, "We must meet the challenge of the onrushing depression," and he recommends so many millions for this and so many millions or billions for that, doing this that and the other thing, and then it is broken down into the various committees, and here we are individually sitting around with little choice once we get away on the President's program to solve the depression.[2]

The nature of a new emergency may be such, moreover, as to tax the resources of Congress far more severely than did the last depression. The chance for recovery may rest on our skill at broad and coordinated planning and execution of public policies. At best, Congress may be capable of no more than the piecemeal efforts that characterized the New Deal. The government must command a steady flow of power—difficult to achieve with a legislative branch subject to shifting coalitions of competing factions. In order to conduct a program of economic reconstruction for the sake of the nation as a whole, it may be necessary to curb the pressure groups, but the blocs in Congress could be expected to make a last-ditch stand against a move to hold these groups in line.

Furthermore, the next crisis may demand of us a general tightening of belts, an "austerity program" comparable to the great effort that Britain has had to undertake since the end of World War II. The distribution of economic largesse in the form of relief, public works, grants to states, and aid to farmers, veterans, silverites, home-owners, and other groups, may not be as feasible during a future depression as it was during the New Deal. Economic conditions may not permit such a broad margin

2. *Hearings* before the Joint Committee on the Organization of Congress, 79th Congress, 1st Session, p. 850.

of tolerance. The readiness of all groups to accept grim conditions and to make sacrifices may be the test of economic survival.

If such a stern crisis came to pass, what would inhibit Congress from assuming its constitutional right to set, on its own initiative, the whole pattern of government action?

First, the difficulty of forging a majority behind a legislative program in Senate and House. Congress lacks the instruments for locating efficiently a common basis for action, for inducing groups to submerge their differences for the sake of a broader agreement. As we have seen in Chapter III, the party fails to fulfill this function. So does the leadership, which has little power to force members in line. Under the decentralized control of the two houses, no one bears the responsibility for a national program.

Second, the perils involved in piloting a controversial set of measures through the legislative labyrinth. Even if majority support has been won for a program, organized minorities in either house can exploit the frailties of Congressional organization and procedure to thwart the majority. Each chamber has an absolute veto on the other. In the Senate a band of dissidents can scuttle the program; even one determined Senator can greatly dilute it. In the House a hostile Rules Committee may bottle up the program for a time, or grudgingly provide it with a rule designed to snarl its passage through the lower chamber. In both houses unfriendly leaders are able to balk action, and if the committees having jurisdiction over the measures happen to be stacked against them, the plight of the program in Congress is grave indeed.

Third, the absence in Congress of the necessary information and experts to draw up economic legislation. In today's society, any thorough-going recovery program, unless it is simply a grant of power to the executive, must embody a vast amount of study and research by economists, lawyers, statisticians, administrators, and other experts. It cannot be a jerry-built affair. But the Senate and House employ only a few such experts compared to the hundreds available to the Administration in such fact-gathering agencies as the Bureau of Labor Statistics and the Bureau of Agricultural Economics, or in the legislative staffs of the departments. In a formal sense, Congress gains most of its information from its committee hearings, but, as Woodrow Wilson once noted, these hearings provide mainly a forum for "special pleaders" rather than an opportunity for impartial investigation, and they have about them "none of the searching, critical, illuminating character of the higher order of parliamentary debate . . ."[3] In most cases, Congress must rely on the Administration's facts or on a sparse assortment of its own.

Fourth, the deep reluctance of Congress to act unless confronted with a program by the Administration. Despite their grumblings, the legislators have come to accept their role of enacting, revising, or defeating the detailed measures submitted by the White House. They do not really wish to take command. The psychology and mores of Congress are antagonistic to its exercise of political leadership. As Senator Pepper said, in the event of depression members of Congress would "all wait around, not knowing what to do."

And fifth, the inability of Congress to make effective use of the administrative apparatus that is partially at its disposal. Many of the legislators are deeply hostile to the bureaucracy. They look on it as a menace rather than as an instrument to achieve the aims of the modern state. Their efforts to control the agencies have a divisive rather than an integrating effect; they usually hold up action rather than promote it.

RULE OR RUIN

SOME may argue that these fears of legislative paralysis are idle ones, since we can rely on the President to fight the next depression. They point out that a crisis will force the Chief Executive to exercise vigorous leadership, as Lincoln, Wilson, and Franklin

3. *Op. cit.,* p. 84.

D. Roosevelt have done in the past, in line with the old American custom of handing over temporary powers to the President during emergencies.

One flaw in this argument lies in its assumption that the President will have the political and administrative skill to lead the way out of a crisis situation. But the main trouble with it is the assumption that Congress will even permit the President to act.

To overcome a severe depression without violating constitutional forms, the Chief Executive must have at least the passive cooperation of the legislature. Congress must be willing to accept his leadership in the absence of its own. It must consider the presidential program as quickly as possible, and if it rejects White House measures it must be ready with alternative proposals. In short, even though the President takes the initiative, both branches must act with a common impulse and in good faith.

Most members of Congress would probably go along with the President in the event of economic crisis. But we must reckon with two groups of legislators who will bend their efforts toward obstructing his program.

One of these consists of pressure politicians who examine any set of measures for their effect on localities and interest groups, rather than for their effect on the nation. If proposals for recovery seem to threaten the privileged status of minority groups, the pressure politicians may withhold their support from the program unless concessions are made. Usually these concessions involve a weakening of the program.

Often holding the balance of power in Senate and House, the pressure politicians enjoy an influence over legislation out of proportion to their numbers. Their strength is all the greater—and the price they can exact is all the higher—if the special interests they represent do not care whether the recovery program goes through or not. In the long run the fate of these groups is, of course, bound up with the welfare of the nation, but often short-run considerations seem to prevail.

For a superb demonstration of this kind of legislative sit-down strike, one may turn to the battle over price control in 1941-42. As we have seen (Chapter V), in a world at war the United States desperately needed broad measures for economic stabilization. The farm bloc held a highly strategic position. Speaking chiefly for producers, the farm members believed that in an inflationary situation the farmer could more than hold his own. And it was clear that the price control bill could not pass without farm votes. Deploying their legislative forces carefully, leaders of the farm bloc fully exploited their bargaining position. The favors granted agriculture in the final act in the form of "parity-plus" prices were proof of their generalship.

The farm representatives are not the only ones to use the weapons of obstruction. The pressure politicians of organized labor fought social security and minimum wage legislation because they were oblivious to the needs of millions of unorganized workers. Miss Perkins has related how as Secretary of Labor she had to appeal to William Green not for the AFL's support of social legislation but to induce the Federation to refrain from attacking it, "for the sake of the President."

The pressure politicians of organized business have waged war on reform and recovery measures that later proved to be vital to the public welfare. Representatives of veterans and other powerful minorities have been equally guilty of the myopia that puts immediate group interest above the national welfare. Can we expect the agents of special interests to be more enlightened in their attitude toward stringent recovery legislation in the event of another crisis?

So much for the obstructionism of pressure politicians. There is a second type of legislator who will use the same tactics but for other purposes. He will be of an entirely different—and far deadlier—breed.

This type is the legislative saboteur. A member of ideological groups on the extreme right or extreme left, he is the evil fruit of social tensions that have been sharpened by economic breakdown. He is no democrat, although he knows how to exploit democratic processes. His mission is to prevent democratic government from moving effectively in a crisis situation because he seeks to discredit democratic methods.

Thus he has a stake in deadlock. He and his fellows, well organized, articulate, and unscrupulous, exploit every chance to delay and enfeeble governmental action in order to aggravate the conditions in which anti-democratic feeling and political extremism flourish. He exploits the legislative deadlock that he helps produce.

Freebooters of this type have plagued European parliaments for years. Can they infect American government in force? The saga of Huey Long indicates the vulnerability of Congress to sabotage. The Louisiana Senator was able to hold up legislative action for days. It was no accident that so much of his obstructionism was directed against recovery and relief proposals designed to help the underprivileged. In the case of the huge relief bill of 1935, for example, it was only after the "Kingfish" had left Washington to make a political foray into the South that the Senate could resume its lawmaking. But Long labored under certain handicaps. Although he bulldozed two or three other Senators into submission and controlled a number of Representatives, he was essentially a lone wolf. He faced an even more adept politician in President Roosevelt. And his career, cut short by an assassin, was too brief to permit his full flowering. A future crisis may find Longism entrenched in House and Senate, more fixed in purpose, stronger in numbers, and unimpeded by a resourceful Chief Executive, and it may find equally unprincipled and demoralizing forces on the far left.

Both these types of obstructionists—pressure politician and legislative saboteur—follow a policy of rule or ruin. In one case it is perhaps an unconscious tactic on the part of agents for special interests who sell their legislative support for a heavy price— and who are willing to withhold that support oblivious of the resulting effect on the general welfare. In the other case it is a carefully planned tactic on the part of those who would pull down the whole edifice of constitutional government in order to reach their extremist ends. In both cases there is a clear threat to the President's ability to act in the face of crisis, and to the legislature's ability to cooperate with him in that undertaking.

THE THREAT OF STASIS

In human societies, Arnold J. Toynbee has concluded from his study of history, "the ultimate criterion and the fundamental cause of the breakdowns which precede disintegrations is an outbreak of internal discords through which societies forfeit their faculty of self-determination."[4] Social scientists differ over the origin of these internal discords, but even a fleeting glance at the daily newspapers, with their accounts of struggles among religious groups, among racial groups, between employers and employees, among producers, among sections, among classes, among ideologies, among every combination of these, is enough to suggest how prevalent and deeply rooted such discord has become in modern societies.

The failure of functional groups in the community to bridge their differences, and the resulting hostility, Stanley Casson has termed *stasis*.[5] "Representative government," says Elton Mayo in noting this problem of stasis, "cannot be effectively exercised by a society internally divided by group hostilities and hatreds."[6]

Stasis is a special threat to a nation like the United States, whose delicately balanced and highly integrated economy requires, in the long run at least, that men work and live together in harmony. For stasis acts on the economy as its physiological counterpart affects the human body—it disrupts the harmonious

4. *A Study of History* (Abridgement by D. C. Somervell), (New York: Oxford University Press, 1947), p. 365.

5. *Progress and Catastrophe* (New York: Harper & Brothers, 1937), p. 205.

6. *The Social Problems of an Industrial Civilization* (Cambridge: School of Business Administration, Harvard University, 1945), p. xiii.

action of the parts. How is such concert achieved and nourished? At one time, we are told, it was induced by the automatic workings of the free market. Today, on the other hand, social equilibrium is maintained largely through conscious collective action.

In the economic sphere alone, this collective action takes many forms. Workers organize trade unions. Farmers form associations. Businessmen establish corporations and combinations of corporations. A host of other federations, associations, amalgamations, alliances, leagues, consolidations, some large and some trifling, some of great consequence and others of little note, spring up in a free and ever-changing society.

Apart from our struggling attempts to establish united action by the nations of the world, the highest level of conscious collective action lies in the national state. Formally, at least, the national government exercises moral and legal authority over any group within the polity. In the United States that government is expected to prevent the organized groups from getting out of hand, whether unions, monopolies, or other special interests, whether regional, religious, or racial alliances. A majority of the people, operating through the political and constitutional structure, is presumed to have the right and the power to hold the competing groups in line.

To fulfill this vital function, however, government must be organized to represent the whole people (or at least a majority of the voters), and not simply the parts. Here we reach the nub of the problem. For Congress, more than any other branch of national government, reflects the antagonisms of functional, class, and sectional groups in our society, and often it sharpens those antagonisms.

Senators and Representatives who act chiefly as pleaders and promoters for special interests cannot perform the supreme task of finding the common ground on which organized groups, together with unorganized voters, may come to terms. Such members of Congress cannot see—they are not expected to see—

beyond the needs of the particular forces that put them into office and invested them with power. They respond to the parts rather than to the whole.

"The dilemma of the politics of economic control," says Professor Key, "comes from the fact that governments must keep in check the pressures of particularism, yet at the same time governments derive their power in no small degree from the support of particularistic interests."[7] This dilemma shows itself most sharply in Congress. Can the House and Senate be expected to hold in line the very interests that they mirror?

It is in time of crisis that this condition has its most disastrous effect. To meet an emergency successfully demands the participation of every group in a united effort for the sake of the nation as a whole. But a united effort also means the subordination of group interest to some common program, and for many groups the compromises and concessions involved in a joint effort are too stern a test of their willingness to rise above immediate interests. Panic-stricken, each tries to disentangle itself from the sinking nation. Like the passenger who, when the gale strikes, grabs a life belt and huddles by the rail instead of manning the pumps, each group puts its own safety before the community's. Blocs in Congress follow suit. Society is trapped in a maze of its own making.

Reporting from France, Michael Clark has described this process at work in a parliamentary system that mirrors group antagonisms: "A substantial increase in production combined with intelligent and stringent economic planning might still, perhaps, save France from wild inflation and financial collapse. But the hard work and austerity implicit in such a solution would require a degree of social discipline, governmental stability, and administrative skill that is unfortunately lacking in post-war France. Indeed, the breakdown in authority has induced more and more Frenchmen 'to get along as best they can.' Individuals as

7. V. O. Key, Jr., *Politics, Parties, and Pressure Groups* (2nd ed.), (New York: Thomas Y. Crowell Company, 1948), p. 204.

well as group interests, obeying a natural instinct of self-preservation, are developing a kind of autonomy of their own, each trying, independently of the community at large, to carve out a private area in which to survive. That explains the incredible extension of so-called 'lateral' or 'parallel' operations of all kinds and also, in part, the present epidemic of social conflicts."[8] A year and a half later this analysis was still relevant to the French situation.

There have been occasions, of course, when Congress has reached areas of agreement that were essentially conducive to the general welfare. The history of social legislation is but one example. And there may be a certain critical temperature of public concern at which Congress must act in the public interest or face disaster at the next elections. The difficulty is that the demands of our complex society and the need for skilled political leadership have vastly increased. Under crisis conditions, the margin for error has become smaller and smaller.

The threat of stasis, then, lies in the hostility among organized groups that is reflected, during prolonged economic crisis or even during military emergency, in a Congress dominated by warring pressure politicians unable to agree on a program of action, and by legislative saboteurs unwilling to support one. Such a Congress cannot be expected to direct a united attack against crisis conditions. The most that we can hope for is that Congress will not obstruct the President's efforts toward national recovery and international stability, or that if it should, the President would summon moral and political leadership to overcome legislative deadlock without violating the spirit of the Constitution.

Which means that, in the event of crisis, at best we may expect a period of strained relations between the legislative and executive branches, with the President pushing a reluctant and wavering Congress along a course of action; and that at worst, we may face a period of governmental paralysis, accompanied by rising social tensions and, perhaps, by a trend toward authoritarianism. What measures can we take to steer clear of this choice of evils?

8. *The Nation,* July 19, 1947, p. 70.

VIII

⎍⎍⎍⎍⎍⎍⎍⎍⎍⎍⎍⎍⎍⎍⎍⎍⎍⎍⎍⎍⎍

Can Congress Reform Itself?

IN 1832, a Philadelphia mathematician by the name of James
Bennett asked Congress for a special act giving him and
his heirs for forty years the right of "steering flying machines
through that portion of earth's atmosphere which presses on the
United States." Bennett alleged that he had invented a machine
"by which a man can fly through the air—can soar to any height
—steer in any direction—can start from any place, and alight
without risk of injury."

The petition threw the House of Representatives into a quan-
dary. What committee had jurisdiction over this unprecedented
matter? A Representative moved to refer it to the Committee on
the Judiciary, but Mr. Sergeant, the chairman, objected on the
ground that his committee "did not undertake to soar into regions
so high. Their duties were nearer the earth." Someone then suggested the Committee on Roads and Canals, but this committee
seemed rather inappropriate, and the House turned again to Mr.
Sergeant. That gentleman was adamant, stating that his committee was too busy with "terrestrial" business to take over "philo-
sophical and aerial investigation." In desperation the House laid
the petition on the table.[1]

Flying machines did not become a problem for another cen-

1. *Annals,* 17th Congress, 1st Session, pp. 1361-1362.

tury, so in this case Congress could evade the matter with an easy conscience. But as Congress moved from the stagecoach into the airplane age, it bumped into other problems that could not be ignored. A nation expanding across a continent, doubling in population every few decades, and shifting from a simple rural economy to a gigantic and complex industrialism, inevitably confronted the national legislature with new responsibilities. In shouldering the duties thrust upon it, Congress again and again made changes in its organization and methods.

How significant were these past reforms? What can we expect of the major reorganization of 1946? Is there any hope that Congress will be able to make the drastic changes that a crisis situation will require?

160 YEARS OF FACE LIFTING

CONGRESS has responded to new problems chiefly by setting up new committees to handle them. Sometimes this response has been tardy and sluggish; on occasion Congress has anticipated rising issues. Shortly after the Louisiana Purchase, for example, the House made the Public Lands Committee a standing committee. The Roads and Canals Committee was established in 1831, although not until 1865 was the Appropriations Committee set up, taking over work previously handled by Ways and Means. A committee on veterans' legislation followed soon after World War I. The Senate, despite its smaller numbers, also created scores of special and standing committees. In both House and Senate the important legislative business came to be transacted in what Wilson called the "little legislatures."

Senators and Representatives have found it far easier to create committees than to abolish them. The chairmen and ranking members can hardly be expected to take a serene view of efforts to abolish their committees with the power, patronage, and perquisites that go with them. Nevertheless, it is remarkable how often Senate and House have been able to override the protests of injured chairmen and to abolish and consolidate committees. In a reorganization in 1921, for example, the Senate reduced its committees from 74 to 34. Some of them were obviously ready for the discard, such as those on the Disposition of Useless Papers in the Executive Branch and on Revolutionary Claims. On the whole, however, the 1921 reorganization was a major step in the streamlining of Congress.

But was it anything more than a streamlining? Has Congress, indeed, ever done more than merely dress up its outward form while leaving the century-old machinery intact?

Even in the case of committees, the reorganizations were hardly of profound importance. The changes made for more efficient handling of business, but they did not alter the way in which policy was made. Today legislative power is still parcelled out to committees that may or may not reflect the sentiment of the Senate or House as a whole, and these committees have a tight grip on legislation. Such was the case a century ago. Were Wilson alive today, he could still criticize, as he did in 1885, the dividing up of power among "seignories."[2]

Congress has not been able to make changes in areas where drastic reforms are badly needed, as in the case of the filibuster, the seniority system, the power of the chairmen. As we have seen, the cloture rule that was designed to curb filibustering has become virtually a dead letter. The seniority rule has prevailed for over a century in the Senate and since 1910 in the House, and despite the intense criticism of this obviously undemocratic system, it seems as robust as ever. The Rules Committee still exercises power in the House. A frank appraisal of congressional reform fully justifies Representative Kefauver's complaint that it has been largely a matter of "patchwork, improvisation, and tinkering."[3]

The one occasion of a sweeping and dramatic shift of power in

2. *Congressional Government* (Boston: Houghton Mifflin Company, 1885), p. 92 (15th ed.).
3. Estes Kefauver and Jack Levin, *A Twentieth Century Congress* (New York: Duell, Sloan and Pearce, 1947), p. 30.

Congress was the overthrow in 1910-11 of the Speaker of the House, Joseph G. Cannon. For twenty years control of House business and procedure had increasingly centered in the Speaker. He had become a semi-dictator. Then in a series of brilliant strokes he was stripped of much of his power.

Following this struggle, control of the House passed into the hands of committee chairmen, various blocs, and individual members. This dethronement of the Speaker was not, however, a calculated move to "reform" Congress. It was essentially a political counterattack by progressive forces under Representative George W. Norris and others against the conservative wing of the Republican party as personified by "Uncle Joe" Cannon. A struggle for power, not merely a theory of congressional organization, was at stake.[4]

The Legislative Reorganization Act of 1946 followed the usual pattern of modernization without basic reform. Once again minor committees were abolished and others consolidated. Expert advice was provided for the lawmakers, and committee powers were defined. Congressional salaries and expense accounts were increased. Touching a broad range of legislative activity, the act made other important repairs of creaking congressional machinery. Yet the filibuster, the seniority rule, the unrepresentative character of some of the committees, the power of the Rules Committee, were left unchanged. Even those who most warmly hailed this major streamlining of Congress knew that the worst problems remained.

ROADBLOCKS TO REFORM

THE men who rule Congress have a deep vested interest in the established legislative way of life. Any attempt at major reform of House and Senate inevitably will mobilize the powerful op-

4. For an excellent brief study of major congressional reorganizations of the past, see G. B. Galloway, *Congress at the Crossroads* (New York: Thomas Y. Crowell Co., 1946), Chpt. 5.

position of the Representatives and Senators who benefit from the seniority rule, the Rules Committee, the power to filibuster, and other undemocratic devices in Congress.

Who are the beneficiaries of the present system? They are the chairmen, the ranking majority members, and the ranking minority members of the committees, who owe their privileges and powers to the seniority rule. They are the Senators who use the filibuster—or the threat of a filibuster—to obstruct majority rule and to gain concessions for their states or sections. They are the Representatives who advance local and regional ends through the agency of the Rules Committee. They are the pressure politicians who find it easier to serve special interests as a result of the unrepresentative make-up of committees. Acting for various groups and belonging to either of the major parties, these Congressmen have a common talent for achieving minority rule by means of the present legislative machinery, under the guise of protecting minority rights. Together they bulwark the legislative status quo.

It is ironic that the devices in Congress which must be the targets of any major reform will be the very instruments most useful for preventing that reform. An attempt to abolish the filibuster would probably set off the longest and noisiest filibuster in history. Even taking the most quixotic view of the members of the Rules Committee, one can still hardly imagine their regarding favorably the trimming of their remaining powers. Nor is it likely that chairmen and ranking members of committees would use their supremacy over policy in Congress to aid those who would modify the seniority rule. The legislative journey of any real reform bill would be rough indeed.

The perils facing even a limited attempt to improve Congress were well demonstrated in the treatment of the Legislative Reorganization bill. Many factors in 1946 seemed to favor the chances of effective reform. There was wide popular support for congressional reorganization. The press almost unanimously favored it, and even among the experts, ranging from efficiency engineers to political scientists, united backing was found to exist. A large group of members of Congress had become only too familiar with legislative shortcomings in Washington, and they were pressing for modernization. Public opinion was so favorable that it was possible to bait the bill with lures for the legislators, such as substantial salary boosts, increased expert and clerical assistance, and longer recesses. The joint committee that was appointed to recommend legislation had such able members as Senators Elbert D. Thomas of Utah, Claude Pepper of Florida, Wallace H. White of Maine, and Representatives Mike Monroney of Oklahoma and Everett M. Dirksen of Illinois, and it enjoyed the services of George B. Galloway and other experts. The chairman of this committee and leader of the forces for reform was Senator Robert M. La Follette, Jr., of Wisconsin, an experienced parliamentarian and widely respected legislator.

But despite these advantages, and despite all the clamor for the reform and even the "reconstruction" of Congress, the bill that emerged from the joint committee was silent on the three most important matters—the Rules Committee, the filibuster, and the seniority rule. Indeed, the friends of the filibuster in the Senate had won their victory even before the battle started, for the resolution establishing the committee forbade it from making recommendations on House or Senate rules. Why the committee failed to suggest changes on seniority and the Rules Committee is not altogether clear. Senator La Follette later explained that the members could not agree upon "workable" alternatives.

Yet workable alternatives do exist. Committee chairmen could be selected by the majority party in the committee, or in the House or Senate as a whole. The tenure of office of the chairmen could be limited to a certain number of years. Or if the seniority rule was kept, it could be modified by a provision that would credit the committee member's tenure only while his party held power in Congress, thus preventing him from storing up seniority simply because he came from a "safe" district or state.

Since the Reorganization Committee scorned these possibilities, one must conjecture whether they feared that a stronger bill could not pass the Congress. If such was the case, their fears were fully justified. Some Senators and Representatives raised such an outcry against even mild provisions of the reorganization bill that one wonders how they would have greeted a real effort at reform.

A section of the bill setting up a director of congressional personnel was the special target of patronage-minded Senators. "I want to bring the Government back to the people," declared Senator John L. McClellan of Arkansas. "One way to take it farther from the people is to put these little page boys under a personnel director."[5] The bill passed the Senate only after Senator La Follette sacrificed this provision. The committee reorganization section went through the upper chamber intact despite the opposition of such Senators as the late Theodore G. Bilbo of Mississippi, who said: "I love the Republicans, but I do not like to surrender so many chairmanships while the Democratic Party is in power."[6]

The bill suffered a worse fate in the House. Among its provisions was one establishing seven-man majority and minority policy committees. It was hoped that these groups would introduce more party responsibility and coordinated policy-making into Senate and House. Since the bill did not change the seniority system and thus left control over policy largely in the hands of committee chairmen who had little interest in party responsibility, it is hard to see how this proposal would have had a major effect on Congress. But the speaker and the majority and minority leaders in the House regarded the proposition with suspicion. Acting jointly, they refused to admit the reorganization bill to the House floor unless this provision, along with a section providing for a joint legislative-executive council, was struck out of the bill. Representatives Monroney and Dirksen were forced to oblige. A third proposal, permitting joint hearings of House and Senate

5. *Congressional Record*, June 10, 1946, p. 6556.
6. *Ibid.*, p. 6566.

committees on matters of common interest, was lost between the leadership and the House Rules Committee. The reorganization bill that passed the House on July 25, 1946, could be described only as a "hopeful beginning."

Passage of the reorganization measure, however, was only half the battle. The other, and perhaps more difficult, half was making it effective in operation. Assessing the results of the act a year after its passage, Representative Monroney found it to be only fifty per cent operative. Congress, he reported, had failed to follow through on what was considered one of the basic provisions of the act—the strengthening and coordinating of methods of handling fiscal matters. While faithfully carrying out the realignment of committees, it had only partially improved its staff and research facilities.

Other observers were even more critical. Both House and Senate committees set up under the new plan were censured for spawning scores of subcommittees that often took as much of the members' time as the original sprawling committee structure had done. Even major streamlining could not rid Congress of its bad habit of splitting up policymaking into fragments. And the appointment of administrative assistants, which the Senate had provided for in a separate act when the House deleted it from the reorganization bill, was dubbed "Operation Falseface" by one newspaper after most Senators had used the $10,000 allowed not to hire administrative experts but to increase their regular secretaries' salaries.

To date the history of congressional efforts at self-improvement permits three generalizations. First, Congress has repeatedly modernized its machinery, organization, and procedure for the sake of greater efficiency, but it has largely failed to achieve basic and badly needed reforms. Second, any attempt at substantial reconstruction of Congress must cope with the opposition of the powerful elements in House and Senate that benefit from the status quo. And third, reorganization victories can be won on paper and later lost to the forces of inertia and standpattism.

BOUNDARIES OF REFORM

To come to these cheerless conclusions is not, however, to offer a counsel of despair. The revolt of 1910-11 stands as a happier omen of the possibility of reform. Whatever the eventual effect of the overthrow of Cannonism, at least the rebels showed that undemocratic methods in Congress could be successfully challenged. Although the job is more formidable today than ever, the best hope for sweeping reforms of the legislative branch lies in the chance that some day a political upheaval will send to Congress a large majority of Senators and Representatives willing to abolish the undemocratic devices in each chamber. If such reform does come, it will doubtless be part of a great popular movement to achieve certain social ends, rather than an isolated effort to improve Congress.

Assuming the election of a Congress that was willing and able to carry out a sweeping self-reconstruction, to what extent would all the reforms within its power overcome the basic problems of minority rule and mal-representation in House and Senate? What are the boundaries of congressional self-improvement?

Congress can banish only those of its defects that originated in Congress. A successful house-cleaning by the legislative branch would mean alterations in the committees to make them more representative of the whole chamber. It would mean curbing the Rules Committee, abolishing the seniority system, limiting the filibuster, and changing antiquated rules of parliamentary procedure. All these were fashioned by members of Congress to achieve minority ends, or allowed to grow by default. They can be abolished by members in order to achieve majority rule.

But there are other problems that Congress cannot overcome, no matter how good its intentions or how stout its will. For these problems lie beyond its reach.

One of these difficulties beyond the range of House or Senate action is the gross inequality in the size of many congressional districts, as described in Chapter IV. The power to determine the size of such districts is in the hands of the state legislatures. Congress has the theoretical right under the Constitution to alter state laws that permit numerical inequities in election districts, but it is highly doubtful that Congress could force the legislatures to reapportion districts fairly unless the latter were so minded. A congressional attempt to correct deliberate gerrymandering would be equally impracticable.

For unequal representation in its grandest form we must turn to the Senate, where one member may speak for over 13,000,000 persons and another for less than one-hundredth as many. Even in the unlikely event that a majority of the Senators were pledged to correct this inequity, they would be helpless to do anything about it.

Article V of the Constitution provides that no state can be deprived of equal representation in the Senate without its consent. Small but self-respecting states like Nevada and Vermont would never consent to decreased representation in the Senate. But the supreme irony here lies in the fact that even the people themselves—supposedly the source of all power in a democracy—cannot alter unequal representation in the Senate. For Article V is the amending clause of the Constitution and is itself not amendable. Even if it were amendable by the regular processes, the opposition of the thirteen smaller states would be enough to defeat it, for amendments must be ratified by conventions or legislatures in 36 states. In short, if most of the American people became aroused over mal-representation in the Senate, their only recourse would be extraconstitutional action, or revolution!

The final problem affecting Congress that is beyond its reach is the election of its members by states and districts rather than by the nation as a whole. The undue dependence of the Senator and Representative on state and locality, as pointed out in Chapter Two, is the root evil that allows the other evils to flourish. No reorganization of Congress within the powers of that body will alter this stubborn fact. Which means also that the responsiveness of the legislators to pressure groups—a responsiveness that is due largely to the power of the special interests in states and districts—cannot be remedied by congressional action.

Recognizing this crucial dilemma, Americans have turned to hortatory attempts to induce locally elected Congressmen to act for the nation rather than for their state or district. Often, as part of their appeal, they quote the classic words of Edmund Burke, who told the electors of his district of Bristol in 1774: "Parliament is not a congress of ambassadors from different and hostile interests; which interests each must maintain, as an agent, and advocate, against the agents and advocates; but Parliament is a deliberative assembly of one nation, with one interest, that of the whole; where, not local purposes, not local prejudices, ought to guide, but the general good, resulting from the general reason of the whole. You choose a member indeed; but when you have chosen him, he is not a member of Bristol, but he is a Member of Parliament."

Unfortunately, few of our Congressmen succeed in becoming Edmund Burkes. The average member is content to play the role of "Washington representative" for his constituency. Even if he should decide to act chiefly in terms of the national interest, he would play into the hands of his political rivals at home who would remind the voters that the chief function of a representative is to protect his state or district.

As Professor Brogan has noted wryly: "The history of Congress is full of martyrs to the general welfare, but any given Congress is full of men who have had more sense than to prefer the general welfare to the local interest."[7]

The basic cause of the trouble is not the myopic legislator. It is the parochialism of American political life and the electoral system that fosters it. This parochialism is so intense in some areas that the best political weapon a local candidate can rig for himself is an assortment of out-of-state newspaper clippings attacking him.

The battle turns into a holy crusade against the outsiders. To

7. *The New York Times Magazine,* July 7, 1946, p. 8.

be out of step with the nation as a whole becomes a badge of honor. The Rankins and Talmadges are but extreme examples of this phenomenon. Such parochialism is not a form of local independence or states' rights, but a form of the ethnocentrism that is at the root of so many of the world's ills.

The question "Can Congress reform itself?" must, then, be answered in the negative. Congress can reorganize itself, it can streamline itself, it can modernize itself. It cannot carry out the full range of needed legislative reforms. The political odds within the legislative branch, barring a political overturn of broad proportions, are against such reform, and even if Congress were able and willing to do what it could, important parts of a reform program are beyond its reach. The common saying "Only Congress can reform itself" is a glib distortion of the real situation.

This is not to say that Congress cannot be reformed. It can be. Nor is it to say that members of Congress cannot assist in the job of reform. They can and must. It is to say, however, that congressional reform can come about only as a part of far deeper changes in the organization of American politics, specifically in the party system. It is because they have recognized the partial helplessness of Congress in this respect that many students of government have turned their attention to the possibilities of a reconstruction of our whole government.

IX

ЛЛЛЛЛЛЛЛЛЛЛЛЛЛЛЛЛЛ

Cabinet Government:
FACT AND FICTION

NOTHING puzzled the framers of the Constitution in 1787 more than the question of how to divide power between the executive and legislative branches. Every delegate seemed to feel differently on the matter, and almost every session in the Philadelphia convention hall saw vigorous argument on some aspect of this basic issue. The delegates actually voted on five different occasions in favor of appointment of the chief executive by the legislature—a move toward legislative supremacy—but none of these decisions stuck. "We seem to be entirely at a loss on this head," Elbridge Gerry said.

There was good reason for this indecision. Remembering the colonial governors, most of the Founding Fathers were suspicious of executive power. They feared that a strong executive would soon become a king with all the trappings of the throne. But they also distrusted legislative power. Some of the assemblies in the states, the framers felt, had succumbed unduly to democratic forces and mob rule. Election of the chief executive by the legislature would be the work of intrigue, cabal, and faction, Gouverneur Morris warned. He summed up the dilemma: "Make the Executive too weak: The Legislature will usurp his powers. Make him too strong: He will usurp on the Legislature."

What to do? Being practical men and students of government as well, the delegates managed to concoct an ingenious scheme that was based on the grand political theory of the time. They checked power with power. Late in the 17th Century John Locke had defended a division of authority between king and parliament. Early in the 18th, Montesquieu had shown how the ancient doctrine of separation of powers could be converted into a self-regulating system of checks and balances among the parts of a constitution.

Influenced by these thinkers, and by the colonial tradition of legislatures against governors, the framers set up a lower house directly responsible to the people, a President indirectly responsible to the people, and a Senate responsible to the states. The legislative, executive, and judicial branches were all to share control and each was to be independent of the other.

This decision was an epochal one for the American people. It gave us presidential (or presidential-congressional) government rather than cabinet (or parliamentary) government. It has brought periodic warfare between President and Congress—a conflict that has become the most serious problem of American government. And for decades it has aroused speculation as to whether the Founding Fathers really made the right decision.

COLD WAR AGAINST THE CONSTITUTION

"SUCH a people," Lord Bryce said of the Americans, "can work any Constitution."[1] Much of our history, especially our early history, bears out this remark. Hamiltonians and Jeffersonians, Democrats and Republicans, were quick to find ways of by-passing constitutional barriers. But wrangling between President and Congress went on, sometimes leading to deadlock. Soon after the Civil War there developed a questioning of our governmental structure that has not ended to this day.

1. *The American Commonwealth* (New York: The Macmillan Company, 1893), p. 297.

Much of the early questioning was the work of the *Nation* under the editorship of the redoubtable Godkin. During the 1870's this weekly published a series of editorials and articles criticizing Congress and calling for a more responsible government. In its pages Gamaliel Bradford, noting that the members of Congress had a "direct and strong local" but "very feeble national" interest, argued that Cabinet members should be given seats in the legislature. Godkin alternately blew hot and cold on this proposal, at one time stating that it was not "radical" enough and that the President must select his cabinet from the majority in Congress, but later coming out strongly in favor of it.[2]

When Charles O'Conor spoke before the New York Historical Society in favor of constitutional reform under which the President would be chosen by—and responsible to—Congress, Godkin reported the proposal in the *Nation* but did not favor it.[3] Like many later critics of American government, Godkin seemingly could not make up his mind whether he wanted thoroughgoing constitutional reform or the simpler change involved in giving cabinet members seats in Congress.

It was to fall on someone else to lift this criticism from the level of journalism to that of systematic analysis of our whole government. In 1879 a senior at Princeton named Thomas W. Wilson submitted a paper on "Cabinet Government in the United States" to the *International Review,* a leading journal then edited by Henry Cabot Lodge. The article appeared in the same year.[4] It was a vigorous attack on irresponsible "committee government" in Congress and a plea for leadership accountable to the people. A few years later the young scholar, now calling himself Woodrow Wilson, elaborated this argument in *Congressional*

2. "Shall the Cabinet Have Seats in Congress?" *The Nation,* Vol. XVI, April 3, 1873, pp. 233-235; "The Admission of Cabinet Officers to Seats in Congress," *ibid.,* Vol. XXXII, February 17, 1881, pp. 107-109.

3. "The President and Party Responsibility," *ibid.,* Vol. XXIV, May 17, 1877, p. 288.

4. *International Review,* Vol. VII, August 1879, p. 147.

Government, a work that was destined to become a classic of American political writing.

The balance of powers established almost a century before in Philadelphia had already given way, Wilson asserted. Congress was rapidly seizing control of the government. The President had become merely an administrative rather than a political officer, and could do little on his own authority. But Congress, Wilson wrote, was not equipped to govern. It possessed no real leadership; power was dispersed among committees and responsibility was concealed.

"Nobody stands sponsor for the policy of the government," Wilson complained. "A dozen men originate it; a dozen compromises twist and alter it; a dozen offices whose names are scarcely known outside of Washington put it into execution."[5] The people had lost confidence in Congress because they felt unable to control it.

What change did Wilson want? Here he was less outspoken, avowing that he was "diagnosing, not prescribing remedies." But quite clear in his previous writings, and implicit in his book, was his belief in the cabinet form of government for the United States. As a first step he wanted cabinet members to have seats in Congress and to take part in debate. But Wilson was astute enough to realize that this step alone would have little effect.

He urged further that the cabinet members be chosen from Congress, that they share legislative power with the standing committees, and that they resign if their measures were defeated. "In arguing . . . for the admission of Cabinet officers into the legislature," he admitted, "we are logically brought to favor *responsible Cabinet government* in the United States."[6] Although such a sweeping change would presumably have required constitutional amendment, Wilson had little to say on that aspect of the matter.

5. *Congressional Government,* p. 318.
6. T. W. Wilson, "Cabinet Government in the United States," *op. cit.,* p. 151.

While Wilson's grasp of the problems of American government was remarkable in one so young (and in one who had never set eyes on the Capitol), his reforms were hardly original with him. He had undoubtedly read the proposals discussed in the *Nation;* he was even more indebted to Walter Bagehot, the English analyst who had probed beneath constitutional forms to lay bare the political organisms that fixed the nature of the state.[7]

In his *English Constitution,* published in this country in 1873, Bagehot had written that the choice of governments facing "first-rate nations" was between the cabinet (parliamentary) and presidential types.[8] He did not hide his preference for the former. The cabinet system in England, he declared, concentrated both power and responsibility in the party leadership, while in America sovereignty was split into pieces. Here responsible party government was impossible because of the separation of powers; the people did not know whom to hold responsible. The secret of the English constitution, on the other hand, was its fusion of executive and legislative authority.

Together the erudite Englishman and the brilliant young American set the pattern of the ensuing debate over the American form of government. Looking back now, we know that their case was not airtight. Neither of them, for instance, sensed the rising stature of the presidential office, and Wilson, as he later admitted in a guarded fashion, did not see the extent to which the Senate was dominated by "vested interests."[9] Their importance lay rather in their piling up impressive evidence for the argument—new to most Americans—that our trouble did not lie simply in "the wrong people being elected to office" but in our political organization, and that the Founding Fathers had not bequeathed us the best possible form of government.

7. For an analysis of Wilson's indebtedness to Bagehot and others, see A. S. Link, *Wilson: The Road to the White House* (Princeton: Princeton University Press, 1947), pp. 15-19.

8. *The English Constitution* (New York: D. Appleton & Co., 1901), p. 67.

9. *Congressional Government,* Preface to the 1900 edition.

The debate over cabinet versus presidential government has come to a head in the last twenty years with the appearance of a series of books and articles proposing far-reaching changes in our Constitution. One of the most notable pleas for constitutional reform was made by William Yandell Elliott of Harvard University in 1935.[10] Clearly discerning the tasks facing government as a result of economic breakdown, Professor Elliott urged a remodeling of our system for the sake of efficiency and responsibility. Under his plan, the President would be elected by the people. Members of the House of Representatives would have four-year terms, and the Senate's powers would be drastically reduced. Once during his term the President would have power to force an election of the House. If overwhelmingly defeated, he might resign. Such reforms, Professor Elliott wrote, would reduce the danger of sectionalism and localism, would make for continuity of policy, would hold the pressure groups in line, and, above all, would bring responsibility and unity of policy.

Later proposals have been, for the most part, variations on this theme. In 1942 Henry Hazlitt proposed that Congress should have power at any time to vote a lack of confidence in the President, who would then choose between resigning or dissolving Congress. In the latter case, the Chief Executive as well as every member of Congress would run for re-election. "If the Executive won the country's verdict," said Hazlitt, "he would get a Congress pledged to support him; if he lost it, the new Congress could itself choose a new leader."[11]

Thomas K. Finletter has advocated amending the Constitution to require the simultaneous election of the President and both houses of Congress. Whenever deadlock arose between Congress and a Joint Cabinet to be composed of congressional leaders and

10. *The Need for Constitutional Reform* (New York: Whittlesey House, 1935), pp. 27-40.

11. *A New Constitution Now* (New York: Whittlesey House, 1942), p. 9.

Cabinet members, the President could call a general election.[12] Frank I. Cobb, Walter Lippmann, David Lawrence, Richard Strout and other journalists have favored changes of various types.

Debate over the issue was heightened in 1946 after the Republicans won control of Congress. Senator William Fulbright, Democrat of Arkansas, called on President Truman to appoint a Republican Secretary of State and then to resign in his favor. The GOP was cool to the idea. Its leaders could hardly view with composure the prospect of a Democratic President acting in effect as a Republican presidential convention.

Indeed, the striking feature of all these proposals has been their failure to gain wide support. Constitutional reform of this sort has been an idea; it has not been a movement. Americans can become excited about political reform, as the history of the referendum and recall demonstrates. But the call for constitutional reform has never fired the popular imagination. The campaign against the Constitution has remained a cold war. The reason is not that agitation has been confined to academic circles; some of the most ardent supporters of the changes are "practical men of affairs."

Are the people apathetic because nobody has popularized the cause? Or because the Constitution as symbol is still invincible? Or because somehow we have always been able to muddle through? Or do Americans sense dimly that whatever the faults of the presidential system, we would be worse off with cabinet government? Probably all these reasons are valid, but the last deserves special attention.

COULD CABINET GOVERNMENT DO THE JOB?

THE easy answer to the reformers is that our Constitution would be prohibitively hard to amend even if most Americans favored

12. *Can Representative Government Do The Job?* (New York: Reynal & Hitchcock, 1945).

their proposals. But that answer is not adequate. The reforms must be examined on their own merits. They must be tested in terms of their own goals—efficient, responsible, and democratic government.

The proposals in general are of two types. Some of them would make the President and his cabinet responsible to Congress by empowering Congress to oust the Executive (through a vote of lack of confidence) and to appoint a new one. The other type of proposal would change the terms of offices so that the President and all members of Congress faced the voters at the same time. Such general elections would be held at regular intervals or when a deadlock between executive and legislative branches compelled a special election.

Under the former plan the President and his cabinet, like the French Premier and Cabinet, would be essentially agents of the legislature; under the latter, the President would continue to be largely independent of Congress and responsible to the people.

The first proposal is designed to give us efficient and responsible government. If the American people ever make the fatal error of adopting it, they will find that it has precisely the opposite effect. It is no accident that this type of cabinet government is synonymous with governmental instability and impotence. It puts a premium on parliamentary intrigue, on maneuver by legislative *blocs,* on balance-of-power bargaining. It forces the Executive to water down his program to ward off the forays of organized minorities. It is irresponsible government because the people are never sure what crazy-quilt combination is answerable for some policy. It is weak government because no ambitious undertaking can be sure of majority support in our multi-party Congress. It is, in Charles A. Beard's words, "hair-trigger" government.

Granting all this, the supporters of this kind of cabinet government argue that the remedy is to give the Executive the right of dissolution. With that weapon he could force members of Congress to run for re-election if they refused him support for his measures. Since legislators do not relish the expense, wear and tear, and possible results of an election, it is asserted, they would not be disposed to combat the President except over a momentous issue.

If the President were disposed to use his power of dissolution, it might be an effective weapon under certain circumstances. But there is every reason to believe that this weapon would lie unused simply because once Congress had the power to choose a President, the members would select a man who had given every sign of willingness to bow to legislative authority. What could such a man be but a political cipher? Even if he mustered up enough courage to dissolve Congress, the organized groups that dominate Congressional politics in the states and districts would return to Washington the legislative blocs that put minority interests ahead of the general welfare. Rather the American president would trim sail whichever way the wind blew; he would ever veer toward the innocuous "middle way" in order to hold the support of the blocs; he would, in short, make himself the tool of those groups holding the balance of power in House and Senate. Even as an administrator he would find his authority undermined by the inevitable intrigues between his cabinet members and Congressional factions. Out of such stuff great leadership cannot be fashioned, and without leadership a democracy cannot overcome the crises of our time.

Even worse, such a government would not be representative of the people. Congress, as we have seen, is fatally defective as a means of expressing the majority will of the nation. On many occasions Franklin D. Roosevelt received rebukes at the hands of Congress—rebukes that under the cabinet form of government would have resulted in his dismissal. If Congress had appointed a new President in, say, 1938 or 1942, its choice would have fallen on a trimmer who had been able to coax the votes of Southern Democrats and Republicans. He might have been a Democrat or Republican, but in either case the great majority of the people would not have received the leadership that they were to find in a man who, as events later proved, had most of the voters behind him in every campaign he made.

How a practical politician would exploit such a situation was well demonstrated by Senator Eastland of Mississippi in 1948. Wrathful over President Truman's civil-rights program, Eastland urged his fellow-Southerners to nominate a Southern Democrat for President in order that no presidential candidate might receive a majority in the electoral college, thus to throw the election into the House of Representatives. "Northern Democrats would still prefer a Southern Democrat to a Republican," said Eastland, "and Republicans would prefer a Southern Democrat to a Northern one." Probably Eastland's appraisal was correct. But if his plan had worked, the new President would undoubtedly have been someone like Senator Byrd of Virginia, who would have run counter to the majority of the people in his views on both civil rights and governmental economic policy. Such an arrangement, if institutionalized in cabinet government, would be anything but democratic.

To assert that cabinet government here would be as stable and responsible as cabinet government in England is to misjudge the nature of the latter system. The secret of the English system is not simply in the Cabinet. It is mainly in their party system. That system, as we saw in Chapter III, provides leadership, responsibility, and efficiency. Without that system the Cabinet in England would never be sure of support in Parliament and would either submit to every new combination of factions in Parliament or give way to a new Cabinet that would.

In a famous sentence Bagehot wrote of the Cabinet as "a *hyphen* which joins, a *buckle* which fastens, the legislative part of the state to the executive part."[13] His words are still true. But the Cabinet plays this essential part only because it is composed of party leaders who largely control the rank and file in Parlia-

13. *Op. cit.,* p. 82.

ment and who can force aberrant members back in line if the situation so demands. In the United States our parties, as now organized, could not perform that job.

The second type of cabinet government runs up against the same problem. The theory behind it is that if the President and every member of Congress ran for election at the same time, men belonging to the same party and backing the same principles would gain office in both branches of government. The result, according to advocates of this reform, would be unified government.

History and logic both argue against this proposition. On three occasions Franklin Roosevelt was re-elected by clear majorities and his party was victorious in both houses of Congress. Soon after each of those re-elections the country was treated to the familiar picture of one branch of the government quarreling with the other. Somehow election of President and House at the same time did not produce harmony.

There is no reason to believe that the staggered terms of the Senators caused the trouble; about two-thirds of them after each of those elections had faced the voters at the same time as had Mr. Roosevelt. Nor was this situation unique with the New Deal. From 1861 when Lincoln struggled with the Radicals to 1929 when Hoover battled the Progressives, Presidents again and again have found their difficulties in dealing with Congress caused not by the opposition party but by factions inside their own.

Is this condition accidental? Not at all. It is rooted in the structure of American politics. As we have seen, the President and Congress are elected by different groupings of voters. The forces represented by individual members of Congress do not add up to the forces represented by the Chief Executive. The gap between the two branches is too wide to be filled by new parliamentary devices, because that gap is simply the surface mark of fissures that go deep in our society. President Roosevelt encountered this hard fact in his 1938 purge. Despite his tremendous popularity and the prestige of his office he was not able to dislodge his Southern opponents in the party because their support lay squarely in places he could not reach.

So we come back to the central fact of our system—our decentralized, undisciplined, disunited party structure. Our parties are not strong enough to withstand the thrust of organized minorities, whether local, sectional, economic, racial, religious, or ideological. Until we fashion a party system that holds minority groups in line, that controls local and state party organizations, that draws up meaningful national platforms, and that "purges" party office-holders who sell out that platform, cabinet government cannot do the job. And if we had such a party system, cabinet government might be unnecessary.

DISSOLUTION AND PARTY DISCIPLINE

So MUCH for the standard case for cabinet government. Some of its champions, however, offer an argument that merits special attention. Fully agreeing that strong and centralized parties are the only means of bracing our political system against the pressure of organized groups, they hold that the President's power to dissolve Congress would lead to greater party discipline. Members of Congress would not truckle to special interests, it is said, if their party leader in the White House could force every legislator to undertake a risky, costly, and arduous campaign. Lodging the power of dissolution in the top party leadership would strengthen the national committees that today are loosely knit and rather feeble bodies with little influence over the party rank and file. Thus, according to the view, what cabinet government would not do directly—that is, reinforce the executive—it would do indirectly, but just as effectively, by unifying the party in power.[14]

If this reasoning is sound, the case for cabinet government here would be powerful indeed. But would dissolution in fact tend to centralize our parties? Probably not.

14. See Finletter, *op. cit.*, pp. 114-119.

True, a legislator dislikes running for re-election. But he hates being defeated for re-election. If his choice is between winning a contest now and losing a contest at some later time, obviously he will prefer the former. And this choice is precisely what would face many Senators and Representatives if the President had the power of dissolution. Most disputes arise between Chief Executive and members of Congress because the former is responsible to the nation and the latter to local constituencies.

If the members of Congress, fearing a dissolution, back up the President on a policy that has kindled opposition in their states and districts, they avoid an immediate election only to run the risk of losing out at a later time to a rival who will speak up for local sentiment regardless of the stand of the President. Actually, most Senators and Representatives will not run such a risk. Politicians are not built that way. They can be expected to spurn his program, accept dissolution, run for re-election back home, win re-election, and return to Washington with a mandate to turn the President out of office.

Translate all this into a real-life situation. A Democratic President, responding to a majority in his party and to a majority in his national constituency, calls for a civil-rights program. The Southern Democrats rebel. The President dissolves Congress and calls a special election. The Southerners of course stay in office, probably having won more votes in the special election than ever before as a result of their mutiny. Either the President remains in the White House, more frustrated than ever, or he is replaced by someone who ignores national feeling for a civil-rights program. That is one possible sequence of events; there are others.

A Republican or Democratic President, seeking to guard the general welfare through aid to free nations abroad, runs up against the isolationist element in his party. A President asking for governmental economy clashes with the veterans' bloc. A President seeking to stabilize prices by law meets farm or labor opposition. To call an election under these circumstances is simply to confirm the power of the blocs. It is to weaken the Chief

Executive who may truly represent majority opinion. It is to strike a blow at presidential protection of the national interest.

To adopt dissolution, then, would not strengthen our parties but would expose their weakness. If national party leaders tried to unseat rebels in the party by appealing to the local voters, they would be no more successful than Franklin Roosevelt in his "purge" of 1938. The local machines, allied with special interests, would hold the trump cards. Thus the effect of dissolution would be to weaken the Presidency. It would, consequently, open the way for a multi-party system nationally, because it is the quest for the presidential office and its vast powers that induces minor parties to join hands with the major ones.

Here again the English example can be highly misleading. Dissolution is used in Britain by the national leadership of the party in power—that is, the Cabinet—to help insure party discipline in Parliament. This fact, however, should not be seized upon as proof that dissolution originally brought about party unity in Britain. That unity flows from forces far more substantial than a parliamentary device. It is not dissolution as such that inhibits the member of Parliament from breaking party lines. It is his knowledge that the party can deny him renomination, and that an appeal to the local party association against the Central Office would almost always be in vain. For on such matters the national leadership of the party and the local organization in Britain, unlike their counterparts in the United States, work in close unison.

Dissolution, we must conclude, is a method of applying party discipline, not a cause of that discipline. A glance at Canadian politics shows that dissolution alone cannot create a unified party system. The Cabinet in Ottawa may dissolve the Canadian House of Commons if there is a split within the majority's ranks, but the central party organizations have little control over the choice of local candidates in the ensuing election. Although the national leaders may try to persuade the local organization not to renominate a maverick legislator, the latter—if he has local support for his views—is likely to win renomination. If he does not, a career in the provincial party may still lie open to him. As a result, J. A. Corry has pointed out, "the leaders of the national parties know better than to try to enforce the comprehensive discipline which grips British parties."[15]

If dissolution works in Britain because a unified party system stands behind it, how did such a party system arise? While this question has not been fully explored, three influences are apparent. In the first place England is a strikingly homogeneous nation. Her political unity is not sapped by ideological differences such as set the South off from the rest of the United States, or by the localism and sectionalism that afflict so many areas in the continental sweep of our country, or by the cleavages in religion and race and national origin that divide large groups of Americans. The English people have a tradition of class leadership. Economic differences exist in England, of course, but these seem well represented by the existing party structure.

Secondly, the fact that the central government has had to shoulder for many years the tasks of the modern state, without sharing that burden with lesser governments as in our country, has forced English parties to focus attention on national solutions and to strengthen central party leadership so that the solutions could be carried out.

Finally, financial control has long been lodged in the national headquarters of the parties. The leadership is usually not dependent on the local organizations; on the contrary, the latter often receive funds from the Central Office for electioneering. Naturally the chiefs in London call the party tune. Moreover, they have been able to build strong national organizations and large traveling professional staffs, which provide information, speakers, and guidance to the local associations.

Doubtless there are other causes of Britain's unified party system than the above. Doubtless, too, the power of dissolution, the

15. *Elements of Democratic Government* (New York: Oxford University Press, 1947), p. 243.

absence of a residence rule for candidates for Parliament, and the intensity of party activity in British life, were factors in the rise of that system, although one hesitates to say whether these were really causes of centralization or effects of it.[16] The point is that the adoption of dissolution in the United States would be a risky affair. Are there other ways of building strong parties here? An attempt to answer this vital question must wait until the last chapter.

SHORT CUTS—OR BLIND ALLEYS?

Most Americans would shy away from the radical reforms involved in installing cabinet government in this country. At the same time, many Americans see the need for breaking the recurrent deadlock between President and Congress. They have turned hopefully to the efficiency experts and professors, the columnists and legislators, who have suggested short cuts to unity in Washington. Some of the proposals, such as that to give cabinet members seats in Congress, are over a century old. Others grew out of the attempt to reorganize Congress after World War II. These all have the merit of not requiring amendment of the Constitution.

Estes Kefauver, the young Senator from Tennessee who seems equally adept at practical politics and political theory, favors a "question period" in Congress somewhat like that in the English Parliament.[17] Under Kefauver's plan, an hour or two would be set aside regularly for the submission of written and oral questions to key administrators. Before a large audience the spotlight would be thrown on departmental policies and practices. The absurd rule whereby General Eisenhower had to report to the

16. For light on this difficult question see Bagehot, *op. cit.*; A. L. Lowell, *The Government of England* (New York: The MacMillan Company, 1931); M. Ostrogorski, *Democracy and the Organization of Political Parties* (New York: The MacMillan Company, 1902), Vol. I; W. I. Jennings, *The British Constitution* (Cambridge: University Press, 1941); "British Political Parties," *Encyclopedia of the Social Sciences,* Vol. XI, pp. 601-604.

17. Kafauver and Levin, *op. cit.,* pp. 69-79.

legislators in the Library of Congress rather than in the Capitol building would no longer prevail. Nor would the proposal shatter tradition; records show that at least one cabinet member conferred with Congress on the floor in 1789, the first year of the new government.

Lavish praise and extravagant objections have greeted Kefauver's proposal. On the one hand we hear that it would make Congress more efficient and better informed, that it would force the President to pick abler men for high posts, that it would put Congress in a more favorable light, and that it would lead to happier relations between White House and Capitol Hill. On the other hand we are told that this plan would destroy the sacred system of separation of powers. One Representative told the House that it would give rise to "bad taste, bad manners, and bad blood" and that "the sergeant at arms would have to recruit a special force to preserve order."

Viewed soberly, the proposal would hardly seem deserving of such warmth on the part of either side. At most its effect would be slight. When handed questions that could be turned to good use, the administrators would try to exploit the sessions for propaganda purposes. When faced with awkward questions, they doubtless would be evasive, ambiguous, and platitudinous. Question-time here would probably not work so well as in Britain. There the Government is arrayed against the Opposition, with all the drama of a contest between two adversaries. Here, too, the affair would become a political football, but in view of the bloc rivalry that dominates Congress, question-time would more likely resemble a football game in which three teams aimed at several goal posts.

Probably the question period would heighten interest in congressional debate. Yet the present system of congressional hearings, with the witness encircled by reporters and photographers and with the subject matter fairly well defined, seems fair and efficient, since it lets other members of Congress, as well as committeemen, question the administrator, without necessarily turning the affair into a Roman holiday.

At any rate, one prediction can be made safely. If question hour should take the place of committee questioning, not many years would pass before the efficiency experts were calculating that time and effort would be saved if administrators appeared before committees rather than before the whole body!

Another short-cut device—a joint cabinet or council—has drawn wide notice. Several years ago Senator Robert M. La Follette, Jr., who later co-authored the legislative reorganization act, urged the establishment of an executive-legislative council, composed of congressional leaders and cabinet officers who would work together in making and carrying out national policy. Backers of La Follette's plan believe that it would lead to more co-operation between President and Congress and would improve the performance of each. Meeting regularly, the members would swap ideas and patch up differences, and through friendly give-and-take they could agree on a common policy. In 1946 the joint committee on the Organization of Congress, with only one member dissenting, asked the Senate and House to adopt this proposal. But it had to be jettisoned to save other reforms in the bill.

Congress might have done well to try this experiment. Yet there is little reason to believe that a joint cabinet could improve executive-legislative relations to any real degree. More likely it would end up as the arena where executive and legislative forces met in noisy collision. For given the multi-party system in Congress, the legislative members of the cabinet would tend to be the chiefs of the more powerful blocs in House and Senate. As Representative Byron B. Harlan has pointed out, even the leaders in Congress "either voted and talked as the majority in their districts required or they were not re-elected to Congress."[18] Such leaders would be neither willing nor able to work in harmony

18. *Congressional Record*, 74th Congress, 1st Session, pp. 1963-5, 2309, 2662.

with a President taking a national view unless by some lucky chance their districts held a national view.

If by some miracle the legislative members of the cabinet came from such constituencies, or if they somehow were able to shake off the clutch of minority groups, the gap between President and Congress would not be bridged. A span would connect both ends of Pennsylvania Avenue, but an iron curtain would cut off the leaders in Congress from the average member who would know that his political power rested squarely in his own state or district, where he must fight his own battles with little help from outside. Legislative-executive cabinets and similar machinery may bring some order out of the babel of voices in Congress, but such devices cannot resolve the power situation stemming from the dependence of the member of Congress on organized interests. They cannot hold together the centrifugal forces that operate freely in our political system.

This point is worth restating because it is central to the whole argument in this volume. No remodeling in Washington, however radical or sweeping, can—all by itself—end the warfare between President and Congress as long as ours remains a free society. No contrivance alone, whether of the "gadget" type or not, will end that warfare. The push of competing power groups is too mighty to be checked so easily. These reforms will be indispensable, however, in the event of a recasting of the structure of American politics. If the political forces that flow through the governmental apparatus can be guided into more orderly channels, joint cabinets and legislative councils will have their part in the directing of that flow of power.

How can such a political reorganization be brought about? Students of politics are becoming increasingly interested in two approaches to that goal. One is by way of the Presidency, the most dynamic organ of American government. The other is by way of the party system. The next two chapters will discuss these two approaches in turn.

X

꙳꙳꙳꙳꙳꙳꙳꙳꙳꙳꙳꙳꙳꙳꙳꙳꙳꙳꙳꙳꙳꙳꙳꙳꙳꙳꙳꙳

Presidential Power:
PROMISE AND PORTENT

SOME time before his election in 1932 Franklin D. Roosevelt gave his view of the great office that he was to assume in a time of crisis.

"The Presidency is not merely an administrative office," he said. "That is the least of it. It is more than an engineering job, efficient or inefficient. It is pre-eminently a place of moral leadership. All our great Presidents were leaders of thought at times when certain historic ideas in the life of the nation had to be clarified.

"Washington personified the ideal of Federal union. Jefferson practically originated the party system as we know it by opposing the democratic theory to the republicanism of Hamilton. This theory was reaffirmed by Jackson. Two great principles of government were forever put beyond question by Lincoln. Cleveland, coming into office following an era of great political corruption, typified rugged honesty. T. R. and Wilson were both moral leaders, each in his own way and for his own time, who used the Presidency as a pulpit.

"That is what the office is—a superb opportunity for reapplying, applying in new conditions, the simple rules of human conduct to which we always go back. Without leadership alert and sensitive to change, we are all bogged up or lose our way."[1]

Here was good history, and even better prophecy. During his twelve years in the White House Franklin Roosevelt was to furnish the "alert and sensitive" leadership that he had found in his great predecessors, and especially in his war-time chief, Woodrow Wilson, who had said, "The President is at liberty, both in law and conscience, to be as big a man as he can."

Roosevelt as Chief Executive tapped all the sources of presidential power. As Chief Legislator[2] he shaped grand policy, sometimes with Congress, sometimes without Congress, sometimes in spite of Congress. As Chief Administrator he bossed a huge bureaucracy that came to regulate and control large parts of the American economy. As Party Chief he pieced together an outlandish patchwork of reactionary Southerners, cynical machine politicians, quarreling union leaders, and left-wing reformers, and made of it an agency for putting over many, although not all, of his New Deal measures. As Chief of State, rising above party, he acted for a united people in the economic crisis of 1933 and in the military crisis of 1942. As Commander-in-Chief he ranged at will through the dark area called the President's war power.

Roosevelt acted in all these roles; he invented none of them. Over the course of American history the great Presidents, and some of the lesser ones, have staked out wide sectors where they could operate effectively, shifting from one role to another as the pressure of events made necessary. It is in the interweaving of these roles that we see the tapestry of presidential power.

THE PRESIDENT AS CHIEF LEGISLATOR

THE striking fact about the American Presidency is that the echoes of the great debates in the Philadelphia Convention over the separation of powers had hardly died away before President

1. *The New York Times,* November 13, 1932, Sect. 8, p. 1.
2. The phrase is Howard Lee McBain's, *The Living Constitution* (New York: The Workers Education Bureau Press, 1927), p. 117.

Washington and his lieutenants were manufacturing policy as well as administering it. And why not? A big job had to be done. Laws had to be passed, money raised and spent, offices set up, officials appointed, procedures agreed upon. Congress needed outside leadership.

Six days after Alexander Hamilton began work as Secretary of the Treasury, the estimates of supplies were taken from the House committee on Ways and Means and handed over to him. Soon the energetic Secretary and other department heads were drafting bills for Congress. One of these measures was the work of the Postmaster General, another—"to promote the progress of the useful arts"—was drafted by Thomas Jefferson himself. Hamilton had a hand in the selection of committees, and even took part in their meetings.[3] He was becoming a prime minister.

There were anguished objections to executive leadership. What had happened to congressional independence, it was asked, and to the supremacy of the legislative branch? "Congress may go home," Senator Maclay said bitterly. "Mr. Hamilton is all-powerful and fails in nothing he attempts."[4] But Congress did not assert itself. Almost all the members had faith in President Washington, who stood behind his department heads. Many believed, furthermore, that Congress could properly share policy-making with the Secretary of the Treasury, because he was as much responsible to the legislative branch as to the executive. And there was some doubt as to the capacity of Congress to act by itself. In disgust Senator Butler of South Carolina wrote: "I find locality and partiality reign as much in our Supreme Legislature as they could in a county court or State legislature. . . . I came here full of hopes that . . . the consideration of the *whole*, and the general good, would take the place of every other object;

3. R. V. Harlow, *The History of Legislative Methods in the Period before 1825* (New Haven: Yale University Press, 1917), pp. 130-162.
4. *Journal of William Maclay* (New York: D. Appleton and Co., 1890), p. 387; quoted by W. E. Binkley, *President and Congress* (New York: Alfred A. Knopf, 1947), p. 36.

but here I find men scrambling for partial advantages, State interests."[5]

In the following years, as some of the Federalist policies stirred up opposition among the people, the Jeffersonians clamored for a return of Congress to its rightful place, even for legislative control of the President. John Adams, with his Boston hauteur and "monarchical" ways, sharpened this feeling. Yet by a strange irony Jefferson's victory did not bring a resurgence of Congressional power. On the contrary, the new President during most of his years in the White House dominated the legislative branch in unprecedented fashion. His power, as noted below, was that of unchallenged leader of his party, in Congress and outside. Our separation of powers had not been in effect 20 years before that great principle had been ignored by both Hamiltonians and Jeffersonians, some of whom had been delegates to the Philadelphia convention.

Toward the end of his second term Jefferson met growing resistance in Congress, and Madison and his successors faced a legislature that was willing to assert its place in the American scheme. The committees and the caucus, which Jefferson had used as instruments of presidential control, became means of asserting Congressional independence. "New subdivisions and personal factions, equally hostile to yourself and to the general welfare, daily acquire additional strength," Madison was told. He wrote to Jefferson that Congress was in an "unhinged state."[6] Forceful men like Clay and Calhoun assumed leadership in Congress, and they were not disposed to yield to any President.

There has been an ebb and flow in presidential power. Following this period of congressional supremacy, General Andrew Jackson, backed by agrarian and labor groups across the country and by a Democratic majority in the House, restored the role of the President as chief legislator. His veto of the Bank Bill was a dramatic token of his leadership.

5. McRee, *Life of Iredell,* Vol. II, pp. 263-265.
6. Harlow, *op. cit.,* pp. 197, 198.

That was not the first use of the veto; Washington had exercised this power twice, and Madison six times. But many Americans had felt that the Chief Executive might justly use the veto only to stop Congress from paring down the authority of the President within his own field. Here was a President asserting his view against that of Congress on a matter of broad public policy. Here was a President saying in effect that he represented the American people fully as well as Congress did. And to make matters worse—from the Whig point of view—"King Andrew the First" was sustained by the voters in 1832.

Jackson's notion of the Presidency survived his death. Even when the Whigs nominated old General Harrison, who meekly agreed with Senator Clay that the President was not "part of the legislative power," the fates ruled that Harrison's successor, John Tyler, was to use the veto as freely as Jackson.

By the time of the inauguration of Abraham Lincoln, who was to stretch presidential powers as Commander-in-Chief, the Presidency had become the seat of far-reaching legislative control. The office as such was deemed—on the part of all but an unregenerate few—to be policy-making as well as policy-executing. Weak Presidents there were, like Pierce and Buchanan, but they were limited more by the deepening cleavage between North and South than by constitutional confinement of presidential authority.[7]

The period between Lincoln and McKinley is often called the era of congressional supremacy. So it was in many respects. President Andrew Johnson, missing impeachment by only one vote, stood by helplessly while Congress seized the reins of government. Grant was at times a prisoner of a coterie in the Senate; congressional leaders went to the White House to give advice, not to receive it. Hayes barely managed to beat off a Senatorial attempt to limit his power to hire and fire. Cleveland, too, had to cope with a Senatorial attack on his powers as Chief Adminis-

7. See W. E. Binkley, *President and Congress* (New York: Alfred A. Knopf, 1947), Chpt. 5.

trator. Is it any wonder that Woodrow Wilson could write during this period that the President "may tire the Senate by dogged persistence, but he never can deal with it upon a ground of real equality"?[8]

Yet below the surface of events were signs that the nation still needed legislative leadership from the President. Nothing showed this need better than Grover Cleveland's experience with tariff and silver legislation. He had wanted to be a "constitutional" President. Early in his first term he wrote to a friend: "If a botch is made at the other end of the Avenue, I don't mean to be a party to it." He added bluntly a few days later: "I did not come here to legislate."

When the New York *Herald* forecast that Cleveland would take a strong line with Congress by using pressure and patronage, the President denied the story in public. He announced that he would insist on the absolute independence of President and Congress. "I have certain executive duties to perform," he said, "when that is done my responsibility ends."[9]

Cleveland's friends were distressed by this firm stand; his enemies—silverites and high tariff men—were elated. But if the President wanted to be constitutional, he also had his heart set on his bills, and he eventually found that the two aims were inconsistent. He had to change his tack. His dealings with Senator Daniel W. Voorhees of Indiana in his second term showed how far he would go in order to put through the silver repeal bill. Voorhees, the sturdy "sycamore of the Wabash," had been an inflationist for almost twenty years and had bitterly fought Cleveland's renomination in 1892. As chairman of the Senate Finance Committee he had to be won over to Cleveland's cause if the bill was to be repealed.

The President acted. Did Voorhees want jobs for his friends in Indiana? The appointments were soon forthcoming, to the an-

8. *Congressional Government*, p. 238.

9. Allan Nevins, *Grover Cleveland* (New York: Dodd, Mead & Company, 1932), pp. 269-271.

guish of Cleveland's henchmen in Indiana who could not understand why the Senator, of all people, should now control the
offices. "You have indeed made me very deeply and permanently
your debtor," Voorhees wrote the President. He switched to the
sound money side and his committee reported the repeal bill
favorably.[10] The "sycamore" had bent like a sapling before the
power of patronage. Cleveland also intervened directly in tariff
and other legislation.

The dynamic nature of the Presidency as a source of public policy has been displayed again and again in the first half of this
century. Wilson and the two Roosevelts were, above all, chief
legislators. Even the men commonly known as the "weaker"
Presidents found that they had to share in forming policy. Taft,
despite his strict construction of the Constitution, took a hand
in tariff-making, although too late to do much good. Harding
promised that he would reject "personal government." Yet soon
after his inauguration he went to the Senate and urged the members to their face to keep down appropriations. Coolidge made
the same promise and lived up to it in the main, although clearly
his breakfast "conferences," where legislators sat down to hearty
New England meals, were planned to sweeten relations between
President and Congress.

At the beginning of his administration Hoover made the customary self-denying avowal that he would not hand Congress a
detailed program. Toward the end of it, amid economic crisis, he
sent scores of messages to the Capitol and used the veto and threat
of veto on several occasions. None of these Presidents was chief
legislator; all of them found that the pressure of events compelled a blurring of the letter of the Constitution.

To describe the legislative leadership of the "strong" Presidents of this century is beyond the scope of this volume, for any
adequate account, in view of the central role of Wilson and the
two Roosevelts as policy-makers, would end as a history of their

10. Nevins, *op. cit.,* pp. 541-542. Voorhees also was swayed by a shift in
sentiment in Indiana toward sound money, according to Nevins.

administrations. But the methods used to exert that leadership are worth noticing.

One method hangs on a slender constitutional peg. The second article of the Constitution provides that the President "shall from time to time give to the Congress information of the state of the Union, and recommend to their consideration such measures as he shall judge necessary and expedient." The Presidents have made the most of their power to recommend. Their messages, especially when delivered in person, gain wide attention with the help of press, radio, and newsreel, and a carefully timed address in a tense situation may electrify the country even when it leaves Congress indifferent if not hostile. Monroe laid the basis for his celebrated Doctrine in a message to Congress, as did Wilson with his "Fourteen Points." Theodore and Franklin Roosevelt both used this device with telling effect on public opinion.

To call on Congress to act in some field is one thing; to hand it a detailed legislative draft, ready-to-wear from preamble to last clause, is quite different. Probably more important legislation was drawn up in the White House and departments than on Capitol Hill during Franklin Roosevelt's administrations. It is easy to find some friend of the President in Congress who will introduce the bill. The source of the measure may or may not be given, depending on the temper of the legislators.

Roosevelt's emergency banking bill was passed in 1933 by members who were not able to see a printed version because there had not been time to print it, and who had to be content with a reading by the clerk. In less critical times Congress is more uneasy about executive lawmaking, yet "must" bills from the White House almost always receive more attention than measures sponsored by the average member.

Another type of presidential policy-making is the use of delegated power. This practice takes many forms. The President may fix the all-important specific provisions of a general statute. He may interpret acts of Congress that are couched in vague terms. He may put some measures into effect only if he finds a need for them.[11] He may enforce certain laws vigorously and let others become dead letters. It has become difficult to draw the line between congressional delegation of power and congressional abdication of power.

Indeed, some delegation is so sweeping that it amounts virtually to a constitutional revolution. Consider the Trade Agreement Act of 1934 and its amendments. For over a century tariff-making had been the great prerogative of Congress, where high-flown oratory and backstairs trading had led to historic enactments. The 1934 act empowered the President to make trade agreements with foreign nations changing tariff rates by as much as fifty per cent. Here was a drastic transfer of control from Capitol to White House.

The Reorganization Act of 1939 was another example of delegation. By its terms the President could reduce and rearrange certain Federal agencies through proposals which should be effective sixty days after being transmitted to Congress unless disapproved by both Houses before that time. Here was a "sort of veto in reverse."[12] The arrangement is a double-edged weapon, since Congress can veto a plan by simple joint resolution, but its chief effect may be to enlarge the President's legislative power.

The President usually has the lion's share of foreign policy-making, as a result of constitutional provisions and the need for secrecy, dispatch, and single-mindedness in dealing with other powers. He represents his own nation; he may recognize other nations or not as he pleases; he almost always holds the initiative in his hands. He shares treaty-making power with the Senate, but from the beginning Presidents have exploited a device that has vastly stretched their control of foreign relations. This device is the executive agreement. Its charm for a Chief Executive lies in the fact that Senate approval is not required. By this method Monroe agreed with Britain on limiting naval forces on the

11. Cf. *E. S. Corwin, The President: Office and Powers* (New York: New York University Press, 1941), pp. 111-126.

12. F. A. Ogg and P. O. Ray, *Essentials of American Government,* 5th ed. (New York: D. Appleton-Century, 1947), p. 300.

Great Lakes, Secretary of State Hay gained assent to the "Open Door" in China during McKinley's first term, Wilson granted the Japanese "special rights" in China, Franklin Roosevelt concluded the "destroyer deal." Corwin holds that such laws not only have the force of law—"they may have the force of 'supreme law of the land.' "[13]

All these sources of Executive law-making are not the full measure of the President's legislative power. His right of veto, his subtle use of the threat of veto, his "gentlemen's agreements" with foreign chiefs of state, his many executive orders and proclamations are among other types of policy-making. It is clear, at any rate, that the President as Chief Legislator has many weapons in his armory, some of them of the "secret" type, some long sanctioned by custom or the Constitution. He has, in short, a huge reservoir of power to draw from in pursuing his objectives. Whether he uses this power for good or for ill rests largely on his opportunities and obligations as Party Chief and as Chief of State.

THE PRESIDENT AS PARTY CHIEF

ON DECEMBER 31, 1793, Secretary of State Thomas Jefferson resigned from President Washington's cabinet and went into retirement at Monticello. This was a historic day—one that, as E. E. Schattschneider has said,[14] deserves to be marked as a national holiday along with the Fourth of July. For Jefferson's leave-taking ended an attempt at party-less government that, however noble in motive, could not possibly endure in a free society. It symbolized the rise of an opposition party.

Jefferson had other business at Monticello besides experimenting with crop rotation and new types of plows. He spent much of his time welding the anti-Federalists—planters, small farmers, frontiersmen, urban laborers, mechanics, debtors, and others—

13. Corwin, *op. cit.,* pp. 238-239.
14. *Party Government* (New York: Farrar and Rinehart, 1942), p. 4.

into a party eager and able to wield national power. Through excursions to New York, New England, and other sections this masterly politician drew local groups into some semblance of a national organization.

To hold full command of his party a President must be the acknowledged leader of the rank and file throughout the country and he must rule the party members in Congress. In both respects Jefferson was party chief. Despite the rifts among the Republicans he held his followers together by providing them with a philosophy and an organization that were to spell victory for a quarter century. For eight years Jefferson was in the saddle as President; he easily won renomination by the Republican caucus in 1804 and he dictated the nomination of Madison four years later. And he kept a tight rein on his majority in Congress.

The control Jefferson exerted over House and Senate has been equalled only once or twice, if at all, since his day. It was a strange role for a Republican who for years had extolled Congress as the bulwark of the people and had berated the Federalists for undermining legislative supremacy. But as Jefferson himself had to admit after becoming President, "What is practicable must often control what is pure theory."[15]

The velvet glove barely covered the iron hand. Jefferson, working through faithful lieutenants like Representative William Giles, drafted some bills, delayed others, and blocked those he did not like. At his behest the chairman of the Ways and Means committee was ousted for failing to appropriate funds to purchase Florida. Secretary of the Treasury Albert Gallatin, like Hamilton before him, took part in committee meetings. The President "secretly dictates every measure," one senator charged.

In taking command of Congress Jefferson curbed the disruptive forces in his party that would have wrecked his grand coalition if they had had free rein in the legislature.[16] His was a

15. Quoted by C. A. Beard, *Economic Origins of Jeffersonian Democracy* (New York: The Macmillan Company, 1915), p. 437.

16. Harlow, *op. cit.*, pp. 173 ff.

strategy that every President has had to follow who hoped to convert a program into public policy by means of party action.

Most Presidents have been party leaders in the sense that they controlled the national party machinery and could either ensure their own renomination or pick their successor. Very few Presidents have been able to use their party as a vehicle for uniting the majority forces in Congress behind a national program.

One of the few was Andrew Jackson. Profiting from the social unrest of the 1820's, the widening of the suffrage, and the political ineptness of John Quincy Adams, the General was swept to power by a new alignment of voters. What matter if his following was more heterogeneous even than Jefferson's? Differences were lost in the glow of Old Hickory's heroic exploits, his frontier directness, his commanding personality, and above all, his democratic aims.

Jackson used patronage freely to cement his union with the politicos who had debouched from local clubs and associations, from committees and caucuses and conventions, to assist him to power. His control of the party extended to Congress. That control did not lead to the enactment of an elaborate program, for Jackson did not have such a program, but it did reveal itself in his shaping of party issues in the lower House[17] and in the dramatic passage of the expunging resolution in the Senate.

Many years were to pass before the country again saw party leadership of the Jefferson-Jackson order. Polk was a strong-minded President who pushed his program through Congress, but he lost control of the House in the mid-term election of 1846, and the Northern and Southern wings of the Democratic party were squaring off for combat by the end of his administration.

Throughout the crisis years Lincoln warred with Congressional leaders, using his powers as Commander-in-Chief to outmaneuver them rather than his influence as party leader to join hands with them. Johnson showed how feeble the Presidency can be-

17. H. J. Ford, *The Rise and Growth of American Politics* (New York: The MacMillan Company, 1898), pp. 171 ff.

come when the Chief Executive rules his party neither in Congress nor outside. McKinley, with Hanna's invaluable aid, had full command of the Republican party machinery, and his relations with Congress were excellent, but his leadership was not tested by the need of putting over a controversial program in the legislature.

Theodore Roosevelt worked closely with congressional leaders and achieved striking legislative results, only to meet growing opposition on Capitol Hill toward the end. "For seven sessions I was able to prevent ... a break," he wrote his son shortly before Taft's inauguration. "This session, however, they felt that it was safe utterly to disregard me because I was going out and my successor had been elected."[18]

It was a student of Jefferson's methods who was to revive the early type of presidential leadership. Woodrow Wilson was, above all, a party man. "The President," he had declared in 1907, "may ... stand within the party counsels and use the advantage of his power and personal force to control its actual programmes."[19] The nation, he said shortly after his election, expected him to be the leader of his party as well as Chief Executive.[20] These theories Wilson put into practice.

Tariff reduction was the great test of Wilson's leadership. Cleveland, with his hands-off policy, had seen the protectionists take over when he tried to lower the rates. Wilson, using his influence even before his inauguration and working closely with his party leaders, was in command of the tariff bill from start to finish. He showed no qualms about using the President's room near the Senate chamber for parleys with the legislators. His lieutenants employed the party caucus effectively in both houses.

18. Quoted by J. B. Bishop, *Theodore Roosevelt and His Time* (New York: Scribner's, 1920), Vol. II, p. 134.

19. *Constitutional Government in the United States* (New York: Columbia University Press, 1908).

20. Letter to Rep. A. Mitchell Palmer, February 13, 1918, quoted in H. J. Ford, *Woodrow Wilson, The Man and His Work* (New York: D. Appleton and Co., 1916), p. 323.

Knowing that organized minorities were the real threat to his program, the Chief Executive put them on the defensive at a critical moment with a stinging attack on the "astute men" who were endangering the public interest "for their private profit." The new tariff bill was a stunning victory for the President. The Federal Reserve Act, the Federal Trade Commission Act, and the Clayton Anti-Trust Act were other fruits of Wilson's talents as party chief.

Yet despite this brave start, party government was not to last long. Wilson's own standing with the country remained high, and he soon was to lead a united people in a World War. But the party as such did not long remain the motive power of government, and Wilson's role as Party Chief became less and less effective.

We find a similar shift in Franklin Roosevelt's administrations. The New Deal President relied heavily on party support at the beginning, with the Democrats in Congress organized to furnish votes for recovery, relief, and reform programs. All factors combined to give FDR full command of his party—his relations with the various groups within the party, his control of a huge pork barrel, his popularity with the rank and file, the aid of capable organizers like Louis Howe and Jim Farley.

Yet President Roosevelt's authority over his partisans in Congress was never certain after the honeymoon period. Control slipped from his fingers during his second term, as shown by the fate of such measures as court reform, administrative reorganization, and wages and hours. Once again it was only as a result of political realignment caused by military crisis that the President sustained his leadership.

It is apparent that a strong President can keep control of his party throughout the country but lose command of his party in Congress. His popular majority remains, but his legislative majority falls to pieces. Yet the strong President finds a way to exert his will even without majority support in Congress. He does this by a decisive shift in roles. Finding as majority leader that his path is blocked by dissident forces in his own party, in a time of crisis he moves into a vast and ill-charted realm of presidential power—a realm of golden opportunity, and of hidden danger too.

THE PRESIDENT AS CHIEF OF STATE

THE role that the President assumes may be described as that of Chief of State. As used here, this term means more than the ceremonial tasks of the President—buying Christmas seals and throwing out the first baseball of the season. It means more than his formal duties such as receiving ambassadors. It covers two other lines of action: that of rising above party and trying to act for the whole people in time of peace; and that of wielding almost boundless power as Commander-in-Chief in time of war or threat of war.

The first of these two lines of action was taken by President Washington. As presiding officer in the Constitutional Convention he knew that the Framers viewed the Presidency as an office above faction, above politics, above the passions of the day. His magisterial figure supplied what Bagehot called the "dignified element of government." Washington was, moreover, a symbol of unity at a time when the new national government needed every whit of authority it could assume. Backed unanimously by the Electoral College in both his elections, he could speak for the whole country. No wonder he condemned the "baneful effects of the Spirit of Party" in his *Farewell Address.* He was Chief of State; the view of the President as Party Chief had yet to take hold.

All Presidents since Washington have been party leaders, or at least party instruments. Not one of them has received every electoral vote. Many of them barely gained a majority of the popular votes, and a few of them not even that much. In other words, unlike Washington, they had no right to assert that they represented all the people.

Yet some Presidents have made precisely this claim. Stung by Whig scurrility, Polk argued in his last annual message to Congress that "the President represents . . . the whole people of the United States."[21] McKinley went further. "I can no longer be called the President of a party," he once said to his secretary. "I am now the President of the whole people."[22] Where were the Democrats and Populists? Theodore Roosevelt, writing his autobiography, said, "I acted for the common well-being of all our people."[23] Each of these three was majority leader; palpably not one of them was elected by all the people.

Perhaps such heady claims are harmless, at least in normal times. In periods of war, international tension, or economic breakdown, however, the tendency of the President to act as Chief of State and to exploit his powers as Commander-in-Chief poses a more serious problem. For, as Corwin has said, "the initiative has come to be attributed to the President in the presence of emergency conditions, whether at home or abroad."[24]

The crisis of Secession in 1861 brought a constitutional crisis as well. Lincoln knew that he must act decisively. The story of his abuse of the Constitution has often been told—how he did not convene Congress until four months after he was inaugurated; how in the meantime he raised and spent money, increased the armed forces beyond the limits set by law, pledged the national credit for huge sums of money, blockaded the Southern ports, and took other drastic steps without authority under the Constitution; how later in the war he issued a set of regulations for the army—a power constitutionally reserved to Congress—and established momentous policies by presidential proclamation; how he asserted calmly that "the war power" was vested in

21. J. D. Richardson, *Messages and Papers of the President,* 1900, Vol. IV, p. 665 (quoted by Binkley, *op. cit.,* p. 102).
22. C. S. Olcott, *William McKinley* (Boston: Houghton Mifflin Co., 1916), II, p. 296.
23. *Theodore Roosevelt—An Autobiography* (New York: The Macmillan Company, 1913), p. 389.
24. Corwin, *op. cit.,* p. 189.

him as Commander-in-Chief, and that "as President he had extraordinary legal resources which Congress lacked."[25]

Lincoln's homely defense of his near-dictatorship is familiar too: "Was it possible," he asked, "to lose the nation and yet preserve the Constitution? By general law, life and limb must be protected, yet often a limb must be amputated to save a life, but a life is never wisely given to save a limb."

All this is well known, but do we grasp its significance? Lincoln was not merely usurping powers of Congress. He was assuming authority that even Congress did not possess. Combining an indefinite "war power" as Commander-in-Chief with the normal legislative and executive prerogatives of the President, he showed that the President as Chief of State could exert almost limitless authority, unchecked by Congress or by Constitution or by party. That authority was safe in the hands of Lincoln, who was a democrat in the largest sense. But never before in America had there been such an underlining of the old maxim, "Amidst arms the laws are silent."

If Woodrow Wilson operated in World War I without the half-naked show of power that characterized Lincoln's administration, it was largely because he had the Lincoln precedents to go by and because Congress obligingly handed the Administration great chunks of authority. Under the Lever Act of 1917 the President controlled the production, purchase, and sale of various fuels and foods, which he could requisition if necessary. He could take over factories, mines, pipe lines, and the like, and he had extensive price-fixing powers. Other measures, like the Selective Service Act and the Espionage Act, vested him with further blanket controls. Wilson also exploited his power as Commander-in-Chief. Even before the United States entered the war he directed the arming of our merchantmen against German submarines, and later he established a mild press censorship.

25. J. G. Nicolay and John Hay, *Complete Works of Abraham Lincoln* (New York: Lincoln Memorial University, 1894), Vol. 10, p. 66.

In World War II President Roosevelt used both Wilsonian and Lincolnian precedents. As in 1917-18 Congress delegated broad authority to the President, which he re-delegated to a variety of "czars" in such fields as prices, production, raw materials, manpower, and transportation, and to "super-czars" for the purpose of coordination. With congressional compliance Roosevelt as Chief of State made the White House general headquarters for the economic battle at home as well as for the military struggle abroad. But like Lincoln, President Roosevelt also tapped a vast "war power" of his own. Clearly seeing months before Pearl Harbor that the Axis threatened the Americas as well as Europe, in September 1940, he gave Britain fifty over-age destroyers in return for the lease of naval bases in the west Atlantic. Under the Constitution only Congress may take such action as this, but the President did not even request congressional ratification of his "horse trade."

Mr. Roosevelt's most sensational assertion of presidential power came nine months after Pearl Harbor. It had become clear during 1942 that the Emergency Price Control Act, passed by Congress early that year, could not hold the price line because of the "parity-plus" provision written into the bill by the farm bloc in Congress (see Chapter Five). In a Labor Day address on September 7 the President demanded that Congress repeal this provision.

Mr. Roosevelt said bluntly: "I ask the Congress to take this action by the first of October. . . . In the event that Congress should fail to act, and act adequately, I shall accept the responsibility, and I will act." This message has been called "a claim of power on the part of the President to suspend the Constitution in a situation deemed by him to make such a step necessary."[26] Like good soldiers, the legislators obeyed this order of their Commander-in-Chief.

26. E. S. Corwin, *Total War and the Constitution* (New York: Alfred A. Knopf, 1947), p. 64.

THE POLITICS OF THE PRESIDENCY

THE fact that the President commands enormous authority in war and in peace has distressed many democrats. They fear that the Chief Executive is headed for absolute power—whether it is called presidential government, or presidential dictatorship, or one-man rule—and they believe that "absolute power corrupts absolutely."

Professor Corwin has urged as a remedy "tying the achieved legislative leadership of the President to the leadership of Congress."[27] He notes that "there is Presidential initiative *and* Presidential initiative—that type which, recognizing that Congress has powers—great powers—in the premises, seeks to win its collaboration; and that type which, invoking the 'Commander-in-Chief' clause or some even vaguer theory of 'executive power,' proceeds to stake out Congress's course by a series of *faits accomplis*."[28] Can we still contrive an effective and equal sharing of power between the two branches of government?

Unhappily, we cannot. For under the conditions of crisis government in America, the sharing of power by President and Congress means the sapping of national authority in an era when our federal government must be strong enough to meet emergencies at home and abroad. The ascendancy of the Chief Executive has not come about simply by chance or through an itch for influence on the part of the White House. It has resulted from the failure of Congress to meet the main demand of our times—action in the national interest. To force the President to share power equally with Congress would be to stunt the very agency that has supplied leadership and vision. It would be to ignore the fact that congressional abdication and obstruction, not presidential usurpation, has been the main cause of the shift of power to the Executive.

27. *Ibid.,* p. 180.
28. *Ibid.,* p. 33.

Obviously the President and Congress cannot be equal partners in war. The legislative branch lacks the singlemindedness, the dispatch, and the information that are essential to victory. Little doubt could remain on this matter after the dismal record of the joint congressional committee on the conduct of the Civil War, leading members of which meddled in military operations, demoralized the better commanders, abetted the incompetent ones, and bothered Lincoln with cloak-room strategy.

Nor can the President and Congress share power equally in time of economic crisis. As previous chapters in this volume suggest, Senate and House are frustrated by their organization, and by the political forces working on them, from acting effectively against economic breakdown. In emergencies Congress tends to fluctuate between obstructing the President and abdicating before him.

Two examples will suggest why the President has often had to take the initiative without regard for constitutional niceties. In 1917 the "little group of willful men" in the Senate thwarted a move to empower President Wilson to arm our merchantmen against German submarines. Wilson promptly ordered the arming as Commander-in-Chief. The failure of Congress to take constitutional action forced a step of dubious legality.

Then we have Franklin Roosevelt's Labor Day ultimatum to Congress, as described above. The sordid story of the price control bill—a bill riddled with favors for special interests—combined with the failure of Congress to amend the measure to make it workable, provided a fitting though portentous backdrop for the President's drastic action. In this case, too, the root cause of aggressive action by the Executive was legislative impotence. Was it perhaps a stroke of brilliant political intuition that led Lincoln to keep Congress out of the Capitol during the first months of the Civil War?

Chronic hostility between President and Congress is partly psychological, mainly institutional. Probably Laski is right in saying that the instinctive and inherent tendency of Congress is, under all circumstances, to be anti-presidential because it can thereby exalt its own prestige.[29] But the institutional basis of the cleavage is far more decisive. It is the wholly different nature of presidential politics as compared with congressional politics. To stay in office a President must gain the backing of the large, populous, urban states, and especially of the "middle class" groups therein. Congress, on the other hand, is dominated by representatives of rural and rural-urban districts and by the organized interests therein, as we have seen.

Inevitably the President stands for more than the sum total of representation in House and Congress. Inevitably, as Professor Herring has said, "Congress possesses something of the dog-in-the-manger attitude, unable to fill the [presidential] roles successfully itself and at the same time unwilling to place full confidence in the president."[30]

THE PROMISE OF THE PRESIDENCY

"THE greatness of the presidency is the work of the people, breaking through the constitutional form," Henry Jones Ford wrote a half-century ago. "American democracy, confronted by the old embarrassments of feudalism, compounded from new ingredients, instinctively resorts to the historic agency for the extrication of public authority from the control of particular interests —the plenitude of executive power."[31] With rare foresight Ford saw that this trend would continue.

Americans have made the presidency one of the most powerful offices in the world because it has supplied the element that democracy must have in order to survive—responsible leadership. So successful has been our experience with the presidential office that proposals have been made in favor of out-and-out presiden-

29. H. J. Laski, *The American Presidency* (New York: Harper & Brothers, 1940), p. 123.
30. Pendleton Herring, *Presidential Leadership* (New York: Farrar and Rinehart, 1940), p. 12.
31. *Op. cit.*, pp. 292, 356.

tial government. Certainly Congress takes on a crabbed and anemic complexion in the shadow of the White House.

Why has the President, originally envisaged as a stabilizing element with limited powers, become the dynamic and creative part of American government? What is the anatomy of presidential leadership?

In the first place, the President can act. In an age when government must be, above all else, a ready tool for carrying out popular demands, the capacity to act is essential. The President's efforts may be cramped or cut short by Congress, his measures may be unwise, but at least he gives the impression of government in motion. He appeals to the people, summons Congress into special session, urges new legislation, shuffles administrative chiefs, issues proclamations and executive orders, calls a White House conference, appoints a new commission. Above all—if he is a Wilson or a Roosevelt—he persuades people that despite his zigzag route, his forced marches, and his strategic retreats, most of the time he is marching boldly in a certain direction. He is at the head of the column bearing a banner, not at the rear consulting a Gallup poll.

The President can act swiftly. He need delay only long enough to make up his own mind—or have it made up for him by his aides. Under the two-party system he is the agent of an achieved majority, whereas weeks and months are often spent laboriously piecing together a majority behind a bill in Congress.

Finally, the President can act on the basis of informed judgment. Elaborate fact-gathering agencies in the major departments, like the Bureau of Labor Statistics and the Bureau of Foreign and Domestic Commerce, furnish data for economic policies. Staff agencies such as the Council of Economic Advisors interpret this material for Executive study. The President follows public opinion with the help of visiting politicians, digests of press comment, and the thousands of letters that pour into the White House every week.

Presidential leadership tends to be responsible leadership. The

Chief Executive lives and works under the spotlight thrown on him by press, radio, and screen. Every word, every gesture, every silence of his is dissected for possible meaning. He must take a stand on most of the important national issues. He must commit himself when expedience would counsel evasion. He speaks to a nation-wide audience; he cannot very well champion isolationism in Kansas one day and internationalism in New York City the next.

When Judgment Day comes on a Tuesday in November, an aroused electorate will flock to the polls by the tens of million to register their position on a wide range of issues simply by voting for or against him. The President helps overcome what Carl L. Becker called "the most striking defect of our system of government"—the concealment of political responsibility.[32]

The President's chief allegiance, under normal conditions at least, is to the popular majority that put him into office. Holding that majority together is his supreme political task. As party chief he must placate the diverse groups that make up any major party in the United States. His popular majority is at once his hope and his despair. With firm party support throughout the country he has tremendous leverage power over national policy. Without that support he is stymied almost from the beginning.

Once a sizable group breaks ranks, the whole party edifice threatens to collapse like a house of cards, as President Truman discovered early in 1948. Franklin Roosevelt's success in harmonizing the many factions of the Democratic party for the sake of a united front in each presidential election was a lesson in effective majority politics.

Partly because he is a majority leader, partly because he is also a court of last resort, the President often lowers political and social tensions by mediating among great power groups. The fight between labor and management over union security in 1941 is a case in point. By the time of Pearl Harbor dispute over this

---

32. *Freedom and Responsibility in the American Way of Life* (New York: Alfred A. Knopf, 1945), p. 85.

issue had halted work in vital mines and defense factories and had broken up the nation's chief mediation agency. Union status was a question of power; seemingly it admitted of no compromise. Congress had failed to act, and collective bargaining on this issue had broken down. President Roosevelt moved quickly. He appointed a new board, gave it power to make a decision, and set the limits of its discretion. He barred the closed shop but implied that labor could have a form of union shop. He put on the board public representatives who could bring both sides together. So successful was the resulting compromise formula—maintenance of membership—that it largely resolved the union security issue during the war. The President, acting as Chief Legislator and representing the overriding interests of the nation, helped ease tension in the industrial world.[33]

The promise of the President, then, is his capacity to act wisely and rapidly, his responsible leadership, his reconciliation of warring groups within his party and outside. Considering the power of the office and the representative character of the men who have filled it, is it surprising that we interpret epochs in American history in terms of the men who occupied the White House? Rough-hewn Andy Jackson and the lusty democratic America of the 1830's; the droll but anguished Lincoln amid the appalling conflict; honest Grover Cleveland and the revolt against public and private spoilsmen; Rough-Rider Roosevelt swinging his big stick against those "heejus monsthers," the trusts, in a decade given over to the muckrakers; the world-minded Wilson and the expanded horizons of a nation reaching world status; easy-going, pleasure-loving Harding, symbol of the return to the normalcy of money-making; grim-faced Herbert Hoover and a disheartened nation—these, to name only a few, are bracketed in the popular mind if not in the history books.

Perhaps the promise of the Presidency is also its capacity to

33. J. M. Burns, "Maintenance of Membership—A Study in Administrative Statesmanship," *Journal of Politics,* Winter 1948, pp. 101-116.

symbolize the posture of the times and to forge a link between the half-articulate sentiments of the people and the course of government policy.

THE PROBLEM OF THE PRESIDENCY

JEFFERSON once predicted that the United States would undergo years of legislative tyranny, to be followed "at a more distant period" by "the tyranny of the executive power." Many feel that we are in the latter period now—have been, in fact, much of the time since the turn of the century. The pivotal role of the President, his unchallenged position as top dog of the whole government, his enormous power for good or evil, all lend color to this claim. Unfortunately, the wrong reasons are often advanced in support of the valid point that presidential supremacy is a matter of concern to Americans.

For one thing, the problem of the Presidency is not "one-man rule" in the usual sense of the term. Most of those who use the term are either making a veiled attack on leadership in a democracy, or they are honestly concerned that one individual cannot run a gigantic bureaucracy and at the same time perform efficiently the legislative, political, and ceremonial functions of the office. The latter is indeed a ticklish affair, but by no means unsolvable.

The President's job can be made controllable by enlarging his staff, by reorganizing the departments for better teamwork, by delegating work to subordinates, by giving the President, in short, the tools of modern management. Measures like the Budget and Accounting Act of 1921 and the reorganizations of the past ten years have done much to institutionalize the presidential office, to make it less personalized, and thus to lessen its tendency to move by fits and starts.

Nor does the problem of the Presidency involve the tyranny of the majority, as we are often told. True enough, as Max Lerner has said, the Presidency is "the greatest majority-weapon our democracy has thus far shaped."[34] If majorities were inclined to be despotic, the President, as majority leader or Party Chief, would probably be despotic, too. But we have yet to see this majority tyranny of which so much is made, even though tumultuous and unruly combinations have frequently seized the state apparatus in America. The "tentative aggregates of miscellaneous elements collected within the loose framework of a major party are unthinkable as instruments of tyranny."[35] In a free society the majority embraces a great variety of interests and attitudes. It has its own checks and balances. The President cannot take an extreme position without risking the loss of moderate groups that form part of his backing.

Quite the contrary. The real problem of the Presidency is the pressure on the Chief Executive, especially in times of crisis, to forsake his function as majority leader and to assume the more exhilarating role of acting for the whole people as Chief of State. It is his disposition to give in to that pressure. Here we reach the nub of the issue of presidential power.

Managing a majority, after all, is a confining and irksome business. The President never knows when some part of his coalition will pull out of his camp to seek greener pastures elsewhere. In the thick of battle he cannot be sure of the staying power of his battalions. He must negotiate and negotiate, compromise and compromise. His majority is especially vulnerable in Congress, where minorities often gain greater rewards than the groups remaining faithful to the coalition. Managing a majority is also a humbling affair. It implies that there is not one possible course of action but at least two, and that the Opposition stands ready to provide an alternative should the voters so desire.

If power must be delimited in a democracy, then majority rule performs that task admirably. The problem arises when majority

34. *Ideas for the Ice Age* (New York: The Viking Press, 1941), p. 390.

35. E. E. Schattschneider, *op. cit.*, p. 85. Cf. James Madison, *The Federalist*, No. 10.

rule, in the strict sense of the term, is thrown overboard for the sake of exploiting some mystical unanimity or general will. Invariably with the coming of a crisis, real or imaginary, cries are heard in favor of "adjourning politics," of establishing a bipartisan policy, of setting up a "truly national" government. Somehow our difficulties will evaporate, it seems, if only we can agree on some compromise policy or candidate and present a united front to the world.

Thus is laid open a tempting course of action for any President beset with the headaches of majority politics. By rising above "partisanship" he can find new combinations of groups in Congress to back up his policies. For the first time in his experience, perhaps, he enjoys almost solid support in the press. Presidential appeals to the patriotic feeling of an aroused citizenry tend to replace tiresome bargaining with party officials.

The Opposition—what is left of it—seems to take on a faintly un-American cast. Such a transition was visible in the course of the Truman Administration. Deserted by the Wallace faction and defeated in the 1946 congressional elections, Mr. Truman recouped part of his losses by rising above party lines and enlisting wide support among Republicans for his militant foreign policy.

Obviously party lines and strict majority rule must be set aside in time of war. Their abandonment is part of the price we pay to channel the energies of the whole people toward victory. But must we pay this price in "peacetime" too? If the second half of this century is anything like the first half, we face a long period of mobilization, war threats and crises, and war itself, as well as intervals of depression and economic dislocation. Crisis will be chronic—perhaps so much so that crisis times will be normal times. Our troubles will be greatly aggravated by potential or actual civil war at home and abroad. Much will depend on the capacity of the President to act responsibly.

As Chief of State and Commander-in-Chief the President will hold enough power during peacetime to take steps single-handedly that would plunge the nation into war. No doubt can remain on this point after our experience in the months before American entry into World War II. Franklin Roosevelt during 1941 ordered the seizure of Axis-controlled ships in American ports, toyed with a plan to invade the Azores, ordered the Navy to "sink on sight" any foreign submarine discovered in our "defensive waters," assumed the defense of Iceland and Greenland, discussed problems of "common defense" with Churchill, ordered the convoying of Lend-Lease supplies as far as Iceland, and announced on September 11 that "henceforth American patrols would defend the freedom of the seas by striking first at all Axis raiders operating within American defensive areas."[36] The effect of these acts was to commit the United States to a "shooting war" against the Axis.

Roosevelt's moves in 1941, in the opinion of the writer, were fully justified. The President saw clearly that Axis aggression imperiled the free peoples of the world. He used the full power of his office to anticipate an inevitable clash. But the fact that the President's vast authority was used on that occasion in a manner that history has vindicated does not mean that that authority will always be so employed. The same power can be used to precipitate a war that history may judge was in fact avoidable.

Presidential power has become a weapon capable of infinite good or infinite evil, depending largely on the sagacity of the wielder. In domestic exigencies it can mean presidential near-dictatorship under the Executive's emergency powers; in world crisis it can mean war. In either case the people may be presented not a choice, but a *fait accompli.*

On the domestic front, at least, majority control is the great safeguard. Once a President breaks away from the majority that elected him to office, he operates virtually without political controls. He may feel responsible to the voters as a whole, but such

36. Corwin, *Total War and the Constitution,* pp. 29-31. See also C. A. Beard, *President Roosevelt and the Coming of the War 1941* (New Haven: Yale University Press, 1948). For a recent analysis of crisis government in the United States, see C. L. Rossiter, *Constitutional Dictatorship* (Princeton: Princeton University Press, 1948), esp. pp. 207 ff.

responsibility leaves him the widest leeway. His actions can have the most disruptive effect on both his original popular majority and on the opposition group. The former loses its representation in office; the latter is unable to find clean-cut alternatives.

Once again a British comparison is instructive. Prime Minister Attlee and his Cabinet took office in 1945 as the instrument of a party pledged to the nationalization of certain key industries. During the following three and one-half years Britain faced the "cold war" abroad and repeated economic crises at home. The Labor Government could have seized upon either or both these series of crises as excuses to abandon the program on which it was elected. But it did not. The government's continued responsiveness to its majority had three wholesome effects: it made possible a steady advance to a viable economic system; it permitted the Conservatives to offer a consistent and meaningful choice to the voters; and at least up to the end of 1948, it helped maintain the Laborites as a united party.

Contrast the political history of the United States during the same period. Mr. Truman's inheritance of a divided party would in any event have made his political life stormy. But the President's erratic course of action threatened to dismantle the party, as he lost parts of the South, elements of labor, and the left-wing groups that followed Henry Wallace. Mr. Truman's swing back to an essentially New Deal program in the 1948 campaign, combined with his hard-hitting tactics, came barely in time to re-establish a measure of party unity and to bring victory. Whereas Attlee was subject throughout to the discipline involved in sticking by his majority, Truman for a while tried to follow an obscure "middle way" that tended to confuse the voters and disrupt party lines.

Our Presidents must be leaders. But more than that, they must be responsible leaders. The great task of American democrats is to bind the President to the majority will of the nation without shackling him as a source of national leadership and authority. We must institutionalize the office politically as has been done in part administratively. Congress has been found wanting in this task, for it weakens the Presidency without stabilizing it.

Can we exploit the great affirmative powers of the office and still maintain teamwork in our national government? Is there a middle course between deadlock and dictatorship?

XI

ЛЛЛЛЛЛЛЛЛЛЛЛЛЛЛЛЛЛЛЛЛГ

Toward Party Government?

THE story goes that Daniel Webster's father Ebenezer, near death in a town given to anti-Federalist sentiments, begged to be carried back to New Hampshire, saying, "I was born a Federalist, I have lived a Federalist, and I won't die in a Democratic town." Later generations are inclined to scoff at such a show of party spirit. Many of us switch from party to party as blithely as we change fashions in clothes. We laud the statesmen who rise above party allegiances and we sneer at the faithful party hack. We pride ourselves on being "independents." The average American feels more loyal to the Elks or to the Legion than to his political party.

The argument in this last chapter is that only by vitalizing our two-party system, by playing national party politics more zealously, and by centralizing control of our parties, will Americans be able to stabilize presidential leadership and foster teamwork in the federal government. The question, in short, is the prospect of party government in America—meaning by party government a condition where centralized and disciplined parties formulate national policy on key issues and use governmental machinery to carry out that policy. This term is used in contradistinction to presidential government, congressional government, and cabinet government, not one of which, it has been suggested above, can safely and effectively master the problems arising in an era of chronic crisis.

THE NEED FOR EXTRA-CONSTITUTIONAL REFORM

IDEALLY, party government works as follows: As a result of winning a majority of the votes, one of two rival political parties wins power. Its platform is attuned to national needs. Its leaders are responsible to a majority of the people. The head of the party becomes President, and other high-ranking party officials assume key positions in Congress, in the Cabinet, and in state governments. A group of national politicians tries to translate majority will into majority rule, and in doing so puts the general interest above special interest.

Since power is centered in the party leadership, there can be no shirking or concealing of responsibility. If affairs go badly, the voters know whom to blame. The opposition party, which has not shared power and which therefore has no responsibility for any unhappy turn of events, is waiting to take over the government if the next election gives it a majority of the votes.

Such a system has obvious advantages. It allows leadership. It fixes responsibility. It harmonizes the various branches of government. It is simple in theory and in practice. Above all, it stresses national action to meet national needs.

Party government has special meaning for Americans because of our urgent need of a way to stabilize the power of the Chief Executive without stunting him. If presidential power is now "dangerously personalized,"[1] the President must be made to share his authority with others. But he cannot share it with congressional leaders, cabinet members, or even the Vice-President when these officials are blinded by particularist concerns of one kind or another, as they often are. He can, however, share that power

1. E. S. Corwin, *The President: Office and Powers*, p. 316.

with other party leaders who are as eager and able to take a national view of national problems as the President himself. He can do so without losing the flexibility of action that must remain in the White House. For the party leaders cannot check the President legally or constitutionally, but they can erect a "Stop" sign or at least a "Go Slow" sign that will have some chance of thwarting rash adventures.

And even more. By keeping in contact with his party, the President can more easily stay abreast of majority feeling during the years between elections. The party, with its tens of thousands of committees reaching into every corner of the land, has the potential machinery for grasping and analyzing shifts in public opinion across the nation. The party mobilizes and organizes political sentiment; the President influences majority opinion but he is also deeply influenced by it. In this sense the party is the institutionalization of majority action.

The best hope for the future of American politics and government lies in a fruitful union between presidential power and party government. The President needs the discipline involved in working with other national party politicians. He also needs their aid and *expertise,* especially as new problems emerge between elections. The party in turn requires presidential leadership to keep it alive to national needs, and it benefits from the capacity of the great President to draw the various elements of the party into some kind of harmony. In short, successful party government must have a sizable admixture of presidential government.

Although they have never seen it in action, American thinkers have often dreamed of party government. Thus Henry Jones Ford wrote many years ago of the "cardinal principle of American politics" that "party organization continues to be the sole efficient means of administrative union between the executive and legislative branches of government, and . . . whatever tends to maintain and perfect that union makes for orderly politics and constitutional progress; while whatever tends to impair that union, disturbs the constitutional poise of the government, obstructs its functions, and introduces an anarchic condition of affairs full of danger to all social interests."[2]

More recently Finletter has written: "The national parties should be the force in this country which holds down the organized groups to their proper functions. They should be the link between the Executive and Congress which enables the government to work in the national interest and against the pressures of local interests, organized or not."[3]

The central issue of American politics today is whether our parties can sustain party government in the above sense. Certainly they cannot do so in their present form. Party government assumes the existence of centralized, cohesive parties like the British ones. Ours are quite the reverse. As noted in previous chapters, they cannot hold their lines in Congress on public policy. They cannot keep organized minorities in line. Led by state and local bosses, they lack central organization. They give little help to their candidates at election time and they cannot discipline office-holders after election.

Our parties show many baffling traits. They form a web over the entire country, touching almost every town and hamlet; yet they are so weak at the top as to be virtually headless. They are many decades old and their names are on everyone's lips; yet as organizations they operate in a shadowland. It is safe to say that nine out of ten voters do not have a clear notion of the make-up of their local, state, and national party organizations; how party officials are appointed or elected; how the electoral machinery works. The major parties probably have more members than any other organization in the country; yet on important national policies they knuckle under to organized groups a third their size. Like the brontosaurus of old, the major party looms large on the landscape through sheer bulk, but it is often at the mercy of the more agile creatures around it.

2. *Op. cit.,* p. 356.
3. *Op. cit.,* p. 117.

Nevertheless, the American party system can be strengthened. It is raw material that can be worked with. Why?

In the first place, no impassable constitutional barrier stands in the way. It is true that our parties have had to adjust to the division of power between the nation and the states, and to the separation of power among President, Congress, and Judiciary. But our governmental forms have also had to conform to our party system. The American people through their parties have established a different order from that contemplated by the spirit or the letter of the Constitution. The parties have tremendous advantages in this sense. Since they are not constitutional organs, they can be changed without amendment. At the same time, they can influence what government is, as well as what government does.

Whether one is dealing with the one-party system of Soviet Russia, with the multi-party system of France or Italy, with the tightly knit two-party system of Great Britain, or with the decentralized two-party system of the United States, he finds that the nature of the parties is the key to the nature of the government. The parties are what we make them; the government, in part, is what we make the parties.

Another hopeful factor is the stamina and adaptability of our political forms. Our parties have had to make their own way from the beginning. The Constitution left no place for them. Most of the Framers feared the effects of "faction," and they set up machinery to dampen down those effects. Even Andy Jackson, some years before he became President, warned Monroe against "the monster called 'party spirit.' "[4]

The people and the politicians, acting outside the Constitution, forged their own political arrangements out of their own needs and aspirations. Their job is not finished; we have reached a condition of equipoise where a jerry-built party structure has linked arms with a faulty system of government. To strengthen the

4. James Parton, *The Life of Andrew Jackson* (New York: Mason Brothers, 1860), Vol. II, p. 361.

party system involves an act of will on the part of politicians and voters today rivaling the earlier efforts of our forefathers.

An important consolidating force in the party is the President. His part in giving direction and meaning to the party in power, and indirectly to the opposition, can hardly be exaggerated. He serves as a polarizing element in national politics. As *de facto* leader of the party, he directs it through the national chairman. Planks of the national platform that otherwise would be obscure, he defines and projects before the public eye. He partially offsets the divisive effects of control of the party by scores of state and local organizations.

In trying to elect him the party gathers its far-flung forces every four years in a massive effort that does something to knit the party together, if only temporarily. President and party are essential to each other; because he must keep his party's support he is subject to a measure of party discipline; because the party needs his leadership it submits to a measure of national control.

Party government can be had. The question is whether the American people are willing to take the drastic steps necessary to create it.

THE PRICE OF PARTY GOVERNMENT

THE price of party government is the wholesale reconstruction of our obsolete and ramshackle party system. The major parties cannot be the means of strengthening and stabilizing national government until they first are reinforced at the top. Power must be shifted from state and local organizations to the national level. Such an effort requires:

(1) A national party leadership responsive directly to the party membership but free to act with boldness and imagination. At present the Republican and Democratic national committees consist mainly of nonentities, except for a few bosses with national reputations. States are represented equally on the committees regardless of party strength. Such an arrangement is clumsy and undemocratic. To be sure, the committees' unrepresentative make-up is no cause for concern because they do little except make arrangements for the national conventions and exercise some control over party funds. Under a centralized system, however, the committees would run the whole party organization, and they would have to be directly accountable to the rank and file.

(2) A small executive council for each major party, composed of officials with national reputations. Except for occasional chiefs such as Mark Hanna and James A. Farley, our major parties have been notoriously wanting in leaders who could think in terms of national politics and the general interest rather than in terms of state and local advantage. The council would fix major policy for the party. Its members would hold controlling positions in the government—in both Administration and Congress—once the party took power, and it would work closely with the majority policy committees in Congress and with a joint cabinet.

(3) A national party leader who would speak and act for the membership. Generally the party in power has such a leader in the President. The party defeated in the previous presidential election has no head. Necessarily it suffers as an organized opposition to the group in power.

(4) Annual conventions acting directly for the party rank and file. At present conventions are held every four years in order to select the national tickets and draw up the party platforms. Since the formation of public policy is a continuous affair, the party platforms should be revised at least annually to keep abreast of new developments in the nation and abroad. These annual conventions would choose the national party leader who would presumably be the President in the case of the party that won the last presidential election. At intervals during the year the national committee or the executive council would have the right to announce party policy within the framework of the national program.

(5) The right of veto by the national party leadership of any

policies of state and local organizations that were inconsistent with the national platform.

(6) Enlarged staff for the central party office. At present the national headquarters languish between presidential elections, blossoming in furious activity only for a few months every four years. Rejuvenated parties would carry on research, publicity, and organizing activities around the year every year. They would command the services of some of the country's ablest political strategists, writers, speakers, and organizers.

All these are among the structural changes necessary to vitalize the party system in the United States. But such a reorganization cannot do the job alone. It can serve its purpose only as part of a strenuous and persistent effort to transfer control of the parties from state and local organizations to the national leadership. All power need not be at the top, but most of it should be. Otherwise the elaborate structure proposed above might have no effect.

Essentially the problem is one of party discipline. National leadership will be a will-o'-the-wisp unless the central officials can read out of the party those who, after using the party label and machinery to gain office, then proceed to ignore the party platform. The "purge" should be used freely against those disloyal to the party on vital public policy. Such discipline need not be administered by public appeals, as in the case of President Roosevelt's attempted purge of 1938, but it can be made effective if the party machinery is properly set up and operated. Control, in short, must be exercised by the leadership through the party organization itself.

What are potential sources of such control? One is financial. Placing command over party funds in the central office would give the national leaders more influence over state and local party decisions, including the selection of candidates.

A second potential source of control is the patronage power. As a matter of settled policy, patronage should be withheld from party members in office who disregard party pledges. It is bad politics and bad government to allow rebels to deal out jobs— bad politics because the rebels thereby acquire additional power at the expense of the national leadership, and bad government because the rebels will give the jobs to persons whose loyalty to the program will be doubtful.

A third source of control might be a moral sanction—"constitutional" arrangements within the party that require approval by the national headquarters of the choice of all candidates for national office and of all planks relating to national issues.

The first two of these reforms might not stir up much fuss, but the third has explosive elements. The idea of handing the national leaders veto power over senatorial and congressional candidates smacks of arbitrary meddling in local affairs. In fact, however, such an arrangement is democratic and responsible, because it means that the party is insisting that its candidates stand behind its promises. It means that the choice within the state of candidates for Senate or House is a matter of national concern— as it surely is. Nothing is more likely to debase American politics than the spectacle of a party's nominees for Congress taking every position across the political spectrum.

Party reform along these lines might do more harm than good, however, unless it was coupled with participation in everyday politics by average citizens on an unprecedented scale. Concentrating power in the central leadership would be dangerous if the result was simply to replace local and state machines with a national machine.

The first step is political education. Most Americans—even those who vote a straight party ticket year after year—do not know how their local, state, and national organizations are run, or who runs them. They do not know why it is that the "party insiders" present the ordinary party member with a choice between evils at the primaries, if indeed there is any choice at all. Naturally our parties have often failed in their primary task—

the promotion of wise public policy—when the party chiefs have been concerned chiefly with the private spoils of office.[5]

After education comes popular action. Voters whose main stake is in the handling of the great issues of our time, whose interest is not in getting special favors from government, must meet and master the spoilsmen in the citadels where the spoilsmen hold command—i.e., in the party councils. That means doing the work that the insiders have done for generations, only doing it better: registering voters and getting them to the polls, gaining seats on local party committees and ultimately in the higher governing bodies, carrying the party gospel to the people through house-to-house canvassing, handling publicity, raising money, organizing committees, and the like.

Those who undertake such tasks in this spirit would find no reward except the greatest reward of all—heightened personal influence over the handling of the great issues that will determine the nature of the world we live in.

Party politics, like war, is too important to be left to the professionals.

PARTY RULE IN CONGRESS

How could Congress fit into a scheme of party government? As presently organized, it could not fit at all. Congress, with its vaunted independence and its power scattered among self-willed committees and individuals, is utterly incompatible with the centralized and disciplined control implicit in party government. The Senate and to an extent the House have always been the natural foes of a cohesive party system. Just as the President has served as a unifying and nationalizing factor in the parties, so by its very nature Congress has embodied the divisive forces.

Under party government Congress would suffer a drastic transformation. It would keep its formal authority as the source of legislation, but most of its real control of public policy would

5. Schattschneider, *op. cit.,* Chpt. VI.

pass to the central party leadership. Individual members of Congress might retain influence, but more as leaders of a national party than as representatives of states or districts. The Senate and House chiefs, including committee chairmen, would be party agents loyal to the national party platform. The seniority system and the filibuster would disappear, and the House Rules committee, ever since Cannon a favorite means of disrupting party control, would become a means of enforcing it. Both houses would be organized to muster a majority—after free debate—for policies proposed by the party leaders. Thus Congress would go the way of "Mother Parliament" in England.

Clearly such a step would mean the end of our "checks and balances" and separation of powers as we have known them. It would change Congress even further from a policy-making to a policy-ratifying body. Yet it would not necessarily mean the eclipse, or even the decline, of the legislative branch. Congress would retain at least four important functions. In the long run, its handling of these tasks might give the legislature a more affirmative and respected place in American politics than it has gained from its often erratic role in the formation of public policy.

The principal function of Congress under party government would be as a national forum. Americans like to scoff at oratory —at what Wilson called "government by the wagging of ready tongues," and what Speaker Cannon once compared to water over a dam—"a hell of a lot of noise, but it doesn't turn any wheel." Yet most Americans see the need for a national sounding board, where minorities as well as majorities can press their claims. Congress institutionalizes minorities by giving them a place within government as a Loyal Opposition. There is no greater contrast between democracy and dictatorship than the vigorous give-and-take of a free legislature in the former and the regimented applause of a paid cheering section in assemblies like Hitler's Reichstag.

A "town hall of the nation" is needed especially in the United States, where minority viewpoints often get less attention than they deserve in the press and radio. Even a small minority, if it has enough local or sectional strength, can elect to the House one or more Representatives who may receive some notice in the press services and in the larger newspapers.

Ideas are far more effective when they are personalized in someone of national standing, whether a Bilbo, a Marcantonio, or a Taft. Minorities should have no right to obstruct the program of the majority. They have every right to debate that program, to urge alternative policies, and—if their ideas justify—to set off "little insurrections" in the popular mind.

A second contribution Congress could still make under party government would be to serve as a seed bed for the breeding and maturing of new legislative proposals. After studying the history of scores of measures in Congress, Lawrence H. Chamberlain concluded that the "long germinative period detectable in the genesis of most laws is of the utmost importance: it constitutes one of the most valuable contributions that a legislative body can make."[6]

Senator Norris nurtured the valley development idea year after year by periodically introducing legislation for a Tennessee Valley Authority, but without avail until it was eagerly adopted by Mr. Roosevelt soon after the latter took office. Here was a fruitful union of minority persistence and majority action. Wagner and collective bargaining, Hull and tariff reduction, Black and wage-hour legislation, Taber and economy, are other examples of minority agitation that finally paid off. Under party rule individual members of Congress should retain their right to introduce bills and fight for them on Capitol Hill and throughout the country.

A third function of Congress would be investigations. Both Senate and House have made much of their power to establish

6. *The President, Congress and Legislation* (New York: Columbia University Press, 1946), p. 463.

select or special committees to probe into various problems; the combined cost for such investigations in the 78th Congress was $767,500.[7] Armed with investigators, researchers, counsel, and the power of subpoena, the committees expose corruption, administrative laxness, waste of funds, and the like, and they inquire into major problems of the day. Some congressional investigations have won great renown, as in the case of the Pujo committee's exposures of the trusts, the La Follette investigation of violations of civil rights, the committees on problems of small business, the Temporary National Economic Committee, the Truman committee during World War II.

Committee investigations are in a bad light today because of the abuse of their power by some committee chiefs. "There have been cases," wrote Representative Kefauver of Tennessee, "where committee chairmen permitted overzealous investigators to violate fundamental civil rights in prosecuting investigations, and to make public reports in the name of the committee that blackened the reputations of innocent citizens who had no redress available."[8] Kefauver cited Martin Dies of Texas as a prime example.

The Dies-Thomas committee has been inexcusably unfair; yet it is a mistake to think of congressional investigations as being mainly concerned with uncovering facts. They are chiefly designed to focus national attention on the issue at hand. The careful staging of the performance, the shrewdly timed questions put to the witness amid exploding flash bulbs and whirring cameras, the answers given under oath, the marked exhibits, the murmuring spectators, all remind the observer of a murder trial, Hollywood style, rather than of a sober inquiry into the facts of a case.

Despite their shortcomings and mishandling, however, congressional investigations are an indispensable tool of a legislature that wishes to retain its right of independent criticism of the executive. The Truman committee during World War II proved

7. Galloway, *op. cit.,* p. 56.
8. Kefauver and Levin, *op. cit.,* p. 138.

that a committee can be highly loyal to an Administration without giving up that right.

Finally, Congress would retain some policy-making power even under party government. Control over vital economic, military, and foreign policy would, of course, rest with the party in power and with its leadership, especially when there was need for rapid, coordinated, and sustained action. Doubtless the party would make decisions on taxes, prices, spending, wages and hours, public works, production, social security, and the other chief determinants of employment and stability; on treaties, commitments abroad, shipping, relations with the United Nations, foreign trade, loans, tariffs, and other components of foreign policy; on the size and distribution of the armed forces, the atomic bomb, politico-economic strategy, and other aspects of military policy.

But there could remain a wide array of matters for Congress to deal with—business regulation, civil liberties, labor relations, small business, administrative organization, the judiciary, conservation, veterans, and so on—which, however important in the long run, do not require the kind of decision that only an integrated party system can supply. The liberty of the legislators to act as they please on issues of this type might be compared to the "free vote" in the House of Commons, where the parties have relaxed their discipline on such matters as A. P. Herbert's divorce bill a few years back and the trial abolition of capital punishment in 1948. In this country, as in Britain, the national party leaders would have to decide when the vote might be free.

In the long run Congress might rise to a new stature under party rule. To fear that its contribution must necessarily be less because some other agency holds major control is an intellectual carry-over from the jealous tradition of the separation of powers.

Lindsay Rogers once said that "the function of parliament—and the fact is inadequately realized—is performed well in almost direct proportion to the strength and ability of the executive."[9] His remark would apply equally to party leadership. The fact that the British Parliament is—as far as policy-making goes —essentially a counting-machine has not lowered its world-wide prestige. In our country the achievements of party government would be the achievements of Congress and President as well, because they would be working in unison and each would be doing its part.

TEAMWORK OR DEADLOCK?

AMERICANS can have party government if they will make the necessary effort and pay the price. To conclude on this affirmative note would be cheering to the author, and perhaps to the reader as well. But the question "what will be done?" is as important as "what can be done?"

The dynamics of American politics are not easy material for prophecy; nevertheless, it can be said with some assurance that we face a period during which the forces opposed to party government will offset those favoring it. Party government is not assured, and the struggle for it will be a nip-and-tuck affair for some time to come. Why is this so?

A major obstacle to party reform is the tight grip of state and local machines and organized interest groups on the existing machinery. The special interests and many of the bosses have a heavy stake in maintaining their hold on the party organization, through which they extract favors and jobs from the government. Their grip could not be broken without a hard fight. So entrenched are these groups today in the sprawling party apparatus that they could be routed not by a few master strokes, but only by thousands of little guerrilla actions in committees and caucuses and conventions throughout the nation. There is no proof that the efforts of the amateurs would overcome the tenacity of the insiders; and even if routed from their strongholds the latter would wait patiently for a chance to launch a comeback.

9. *Crisis Government* (New York: W. W. Norton, 1934), p. 117.

Another stumbling-block is the fact that party government could not be sold as a cure-all. It must compete with reforms that are thought by their sponsors to be panaceas. For all the good that it would do, party rule would not solve such obvious problems as the two-thirds vote required in the Senate for ratifying treaties, the difficulty of amending the Constitution, and the power of judicial veto. On the contrary, party government would bring new issues in its wake. The proper relationship between the President and the other party leaders, for example, could not easily be defined, and there would be major questions of stabilizing and delimiting power within the party structure.

Many Americans, in fact, would look on party cohesion and discipline as wholly alien to our traditional ways of carrying on politics. Centralized government seems bad enough; centralized parties might seem even worse. This attitude is not surprising, because the present arrangements fit nicely the individualistic culture and the loose social and political structure of American society, and it is likely that party reform would upset customary political practices.

Concentrating power at the national level of the party smacks of the one-party system in totalitarian states, and there would indeed be a superficial similarity between the one-party systems abroad and a centralized party system here, as there is between the structure of the British parties and that of the Communist party in Soviet Russia. The main difference—and it is a crucial one—lies in the fact that the totalitarians have one party and we have at least two. That fact is simple, but not necessarily obvious.

The main bar to the development of party government is intellectual, as Schattschneider has noted.[10] Not only are Americans generally in the dark as to the nature of both the problem and the solution, but social scientists are widely split over the best way to strengthen our government. That changes must be made they usually agree, but recommendations run all the way from minor tinkering to the most drastic alterations of the Con-

10. *Op cit.,* p. 209.

stitution. This disagreement over means stems in large part from differences over ends.

An example of the prevailing confusion in the popular mind is the fact that the nature of the real problem has been obscured by the din over the question: Why don't the major parties stand for different programs? This question is important, but it implies that in this area the relations between the major parties, rather than their internal organization, is the real issue. The opposite is the case. Naturally parties straddle issues when they try to sit astride diverse groups. They will continue to be everything to everyone as long as their loose organization permits diverse groups to work through either or both parties in pursuit of their minority objectives.

Parties will come to stand for relatively clear-cut programs only if there is discipline at the top to enforce each party's platform and to keep the whole organization alert and flexible in the face of new conditions. In Pendleton Herring's words, the parties' "highest function is to readjust existing forces into more effective patterns for action."[11]

The obstacles to party government, then, are both political and intellectual. What are the forces working in the other direction—in favor of party reform?

One is the changing role of some of the city machines. The boss who used to buy votes with a Christmas basket or a sack of potatoes has had to fight for survival in a day when government provides welfare services and social legislation on a vast scale. Local party leaders have reaped votes by supporting the new dispensation rather than resisting it. It is not accidental that Tammany, elements of which hated Franklin Roosevelt, backed him noisily at election time and rode its local candidates into office on his long coat tails. Or that congressmen from many of the city machines went "down the line" for New Deal measures. Or that leaders like Ed Flynn of the Bronx and Jake Arvey of Chicago

11. *The Politics of Democracy* (New York: W. W. Norton, 1940), p. 191.

stress the need today for a progressive Democratic party. The big-city bosses may insist on party unity and action as the price of their own survival.[12]

Another force for party government is heightened concern on the part of millions of voters over the handling of national issues —the Bomb, economic and military aid to foreign nations, full employment, civil rights, social legislation. Since this type of problem cannot be solved locally, perhaps more voters will work in their parties to make them better instruments for facing such problems on the national level.

Hope can also be found in the awareness of groups like the League of Women Voters and Americans for Democratic Action that the individual is more effective politically as a party member than as an independent.

Finally, there is the influence of the President. He has a centralizing effect on the party, especially, as noted above, when he exercises vigorous leadership in behalf of his program. But that effect can be a fleeting one, as we saw after Franklin Roosevelt's death. And a major question remains as to whether strengthening the President in the long run will help centralize the party, or whether strengthening the President will be an easy way of by-passing party rule in order to avoid paying its heavy price.

No one can safely predict the outcome of the struggle for party government.[13] But one thing seems likely. That struggle will shape much of the course of government during the coming generation. And it will show itself sooner or later in President Truman's second Administration.

Mr. Truman confronts a Congress composed basically of the same forces that dominated it during Franklin Roosevelt's later years in office. Perhaps a third of the legislators are liberal Democrats, a large minority are Republicans, and the remainder—

12. See H. R. Penniman, *Sait's American Parties and Elections* (4th ed.) (New York: Appleton-Century-Crofts, 1948), pp. 376-378.

13. See also E. E. Schattschneider, *The Struggle for Party Government,* University of Maryland, 1948. A committee of the American Political Science Association has been studying the problems of the American party system.

holding the balance of power—are conservative Democrats, mainly from the South. Many important House and Senate committees are back under the chairmanship of "Old Guard" Democrats from safe districts.

Once again Congress is on trial. In the 1948 election Mr. Truman evidently won endorsement for an internationalist foreign policy and a liberal domestic policy after he had vigorously taken his case to voters across the land. Following his stunning victory he asserted that he would make good on his promises of housing, civil rights, extended social legislation, inflation control, and readiness to meet the threat of boom-and-bust.

Many members of Congress had not made these promises or had simply paid them lip-service. Others would go along with new legislation as long as it did not seem to endanger various interests back home. Mr. Truman was not granted even the usual honeymoon permitted by Congress at the start of presidential terms. Ultimately the gulf between White House and Capitol Hill is bound to show itself.

If Mr. Truman and his successors fail to act as party leaders, if a more unified party system is not achieved, the pattern of American politics during the next few decades can be foreseen, at least in rough outline.

"In the Archey Road," Mr. Dooley once observed, "when a man and woman find they simply can't go on living together—they go on living together." So will Congress and the President. But in the absence of party unity, wedlock would continue to be unhappy and unfruitful. It would not yield the teamwork in government that we sorely need. Rather we could expect recurrent periods of deadlock as Congress and the President wrestled for supremacy, ending in shifts to presidential rule as the people in time of crisis called for action—any action. Could our democracy stand the strain?

Bibliography

APPLEBY, PAUL H. *Big Democracy*. New York: A. A. Knopf, 1945, Pp. viii+197.

BECKER, CARL L. *Freedom and Responsibility in the American Way of Life*. New York: A. A. Knopf, 1945. Pp. xlii+122.

BINKLEY, WILFRED E. *American Political Parties: Their Natural History*. 2nd ed. New York: A. A. Knopf, 1947. Pp. xi+420.

——. *President and Congress*. New York: A. A. Knopf, 1947. Pp. viii+312.

BLAISDELL, DONALD C. *Government Under Pressure*. New York: Public Affairs Committee, 1942. Pp. 31.

BURDETTE, F. L. *Filibustering in the Senate*. Princeton: Princeton University Press, 1940. Pp. ix+252.

CHAMBERLAIN, LAWRENCE H. *The President, Congress, and Legislation*. New York: Columbia University Press, 1946. Pp. 478.

COMMAGER, HENRY S. *Majority Rule and Minority Rights*. New York: Oxford University Press, 1943. Pp. 92.

CORWIN, EDWARD S. *The President: Office and Powers*. New York: New York University Press, 1940. Pp. xiii+476.

CUSHMAN, R. E. *The Independent Regulatory Commissions*. New York: Oxford University Press, 1941. Pp. xiv+780.

ELLIOTT, WILLIAM Y. *The Need for Constitutional Reform*. New York: Whittlesey House, 1935. Pp. x+286.

FINLETTER, THOMAS K. *Can Representative Government Do the Job?* New York: Reynal & Hitchcock, 1945. Pp. 184.

FOLLETT, MARY P. *The Speaker of the House of Representatives*. New York: Longmans, Green & Co., 1896. Pp. xxvi+378.

FORD, HENRY JONES. *The Rise and Growth of American Politics*. New York: The MacMillan Co., 1898. Pp. viii+409.

FRIEDRICH, CARL J. *Constitutional Government and Democracy.* Boston: Ginn & Co., 1946. Pp. xix+695.

GALLOWAY, GEORGE B. *Congress at the Crossroads.* New York: Thomas Y. Crowell Co., 1946. Pp. ix+374.

HARLOW, RALPH V. *The History of Legislative Methods in the Period Before 1825.* New Haven: Yale University Press, 1917. Pp. x+269.

HAZLITT, HENRY. *A New Constitution Now.* New York: Whittlesey House, 1942. Pp. xiii+297.

HELLER, ROBERT. *Strengthening the Congress.* Washington: National Planning Assn., 1947. Pp. vi+17.

HERRING, PENDLETON. *The Politics of Democracy.* New York: W. W. Norton & Co., 1940. Pp. xx+468.

――――. *Presidential Leadership.* New York: Farrar & Rinehart, 1940. Pp. xiv+173.

――――. *Public Administration and the Public Interest.* New York: McGraw Hill Book Co., 1936. Pp. xii+416.

HOLCOMBE, ARTHUR N. *Government in a Planned Democracy.* New York: W. W. Norton & Co., 1935. Pp. ix+173.

――――. *The Middle Classes in American Politics.* Cambridge, Mass.: Harvard University Press, 1940. Pp. vi+304.

JENNINGS, W. IVOR. *Parliament.* New York: The MacMillan Co., 1940. Pp. xiii+548.

KEFAUVER, ESTES and LEVIN, JACK. *20th Century Congress.* New York: Duell, Sloan, & Pearce, 1947. Pp. xiv+236.

KEY, V. O., JR. *Politics, Parties, and Pressure Groups.* 2nd ed. New York: Thomas Y. Crowell Co., 1948. Pp. xvi+767.

LASKI, HAROLD J. *The American Presidency.* New York: Harper & Brothers, 1940. Pp. viii+278.

――――. *Parliamentary Government in England.* New York: The Viking Press, 1938. Pp. 383.

LAZARSFELD, P. F. et al. *The People's Choice.* New York: Duell, Sloan, & Pearce, 1944. Pp. vii+178.

LERNER, MAX. *Ideas Are Weapons.* New York: The Viking Press, 1939. Pp. xiv+553.

――――. *Ideas for the Ice Age.* New York: The Viking Press, 1941. Pp. xiii+432.

LUCE, ROBERT. *Congress: An Explanation.* Cambridge, Mass.: Harvard University Press, 1926. Pp. 154.

ODEGARD, PETER H. and HELMS, E. ALLEN. *American Politics.* 2nd ed. New York: Harper & Brothers, 1947. Pp. xiii+896.

OSTROGORSKI, M. *Democracy and the Organization of Political Parties.* New York: The MacMillan Co., 1902. 2 vol.

The Reorganization of Congress. A Report of the Committee on Congress of the American Political Science Association. Washington, D. C.: Public Affairs Press, 1945. Pp. 89.

ROBINSON, EDGAR E. *The Evolution of American Political Parties.* New York: Harcourt, Brace & Co., 1924. Pp. viii+382.

ROGERS, LINDSAY. *The American Senate.* New York: A. A. Knopf, 1926. Pp. xii+285.

———. *Crisis Government.* New York: W. W. Norton & Co., 1934. Pp. 166.

SCHATTSCHNEIDER, E. E. *Party Government.* New York: Farrar & Rinehart, 1942. Pp. xv+219.

———. *Politics, Pressures, and the Tariff.* New York: Prentice-Hall Inc., 1935. Pp. xi+301.

SMITH, T. V. *The Legislative Way of Life.* Chicago, Ill.: University of Chicago Press, 1940. Pp. xi+101.

TORREY, VOLTA. *You and Your Congress.* New York: W. Morrow & Co., 1944. Pp. vii+280.

WALKER, HARVEY. *Law Making in the United States.* New York: The Ronald Press, 1934. Pp. x+495.

WILSON, WOODROW. *Congressional Government.* 9th ed. Boston: Houghton, Mifflin & Co., 1892. Pp. 344.

WILLOUGHBY, W. F. *Principles of Legislative Organization and Administration.* Washington, D. C.: The Brookings Institution, 1934. Pp. xiv+657.

YOUNG, ROLAND A. *This Is Congress.* 2nd ed. New York: A. A. Knopf, 1946. Pp. xx+267.

Index